GUSTAV STICKLEY
The Craftsman

A New York State Study

Gustav Stickley, c. 1909. *Craftsman Homes* (New York: Craftsman Publishing Co., 1909).

GUSTAV STICKLEY
The Craftsman

MARY ANN SMITH

SYRACUSE UNIVERSITY PRESS

1983

This book is published with the assistance of a grant
from the John Ben Snow Foundation.

Library of Congress Cataloging in Publication Data

Smith, Mary Ann, 1934–
Gustav Stickley, the craftsman.

(A New York State Study)
Includes Biographical References and Index.
1. Stickley, Gustav, 1858–1942.   I. Title.
N6537.S74S6   1983   728.3′7′0924   82-19538
ISBN 0-8156-2293-7

Manufactured in the United States of America

CONTENTS

Mary Ann Smith received an M.A. from the University of North Carolina, Chapel Hill, and a Ph.D. from Pennsylvania State University. She has published articles in *The Tiller, Nineteenth Century,* and *New-York Historical Society Quarterly* and is Associate Professor of Architecture at Syracuse University. Her special interests are American architecture and its preservation.

PREFACE

T THE BEGINNING of the twentieth century, Gustav Stickley modestly introduced a radically new kind of furniture to the American public. From his headquarters in central New York State, he soon expanded his furniture manufacturing activities to include publication of *The Craftsman* magazine which led to his involvement in furniture design. In recent years Gustav Stickley's contributions to the American Arts and Crafts Movement have been gradually rediscovered. John Crosby Freeman led the way with his book, *Forgotten Rebel: Gustav Stickley and His Craftsman Mission Furniture* (1966), which has served as a basic source for Stickley scholars. In 1972, a major exhibition held at Princeton and its well-illustrated catalog, *The Arts and Crafts Movement in America 1876–1916,* contributed to a renewal of interest in important designers of furniture, ceramics, metalwork, and books during the period between 1876 and 1916. Gustav Stickley was mentioned in more different categories than any other person in the Princeton catalog, being represented in every field except ceramics. His contributions in architecture were beyond the limits of the exhibition. More recently, reprint editions of Stickley's Craftsman house books, Craftsman furniture catalogs, and excerpts from his *Craftsman* magazine have appeared, as have a book and many articles about his Craftsman furniture. His furniture has received so much attention that his other design activities have been almost overlooked.

Even with all these publications, there has not been a serious study of the totality of Stickley's accomplishments. Logically these should be considered as parts of a whole since the energetic Gustav Stickley was active in furniture design, publishing, and architecture during most of his career within the Movement. Indeed, involvement in the totality of the design spectrum was one of the important ideas he derived from the English Arts and Crafts example. Therefore, this book is an effort to put Stickley's many accomplishments into perspective and to explore his complementary interests as they aided in the formulation of a utopian Arts and Crafts philosophy and lifestyle.

I have chosen to emphasize his architectural achievements because this important area of his work has been largely unstudied by others. The Craftsman house, so logically the extension of his furniture designs, is the summation of his Arts and Crafts philosophy. Dedicated Craftsman furniture customers who presumably read Stickley's *Craftsman* magazine built Craftsman houses complete with Craftsman light fixtures, hardware, and woodwork. These customers could even purchase Craftsman linens and rugs selected by Stickley to complete the Craftsman house interior.

Although I have discovered a number of Craftsman houses, further research will certainly document others. Since there is no source of the names and addresses of all those people who ordered Craftsman plans to build their dream houses, documentation is difficult. Even though many American houses built prior to World War I resemble Craftsman designs, the true Craftsman house, once seen, is easy to identify because of its absolutely forthright, honest expression of structure and the clarity of its interior design. The street addresses of the Craftsman houses used as examples in this study have been omitted in order to preserve the privacy of their owners.

I have attempted to set the record straight on various small errors in Stickley research and to place Stickley within the design context of his time. He was not the only important figure in the American Arts and Crafts Movement although vitally important as its chief publicist. I have treated Stickley neither as an antimodernist nor as a precursor of the modern movement but rather as a man of his own time. There were certainly antimodernist and modernist tendencies in his work.

Many people have provided help and inspiration for this study. First is Dr. Harold Dickson, Professor Emeritus, Pennsylvania State University, who suggested almost twenty years ago that "somebody ought to find out about Gustav Stickley" and taught me enough about Stickley to inspire additional research. I am grateful to him.

I am indebted to the following librarians for their help and interest in this project: Janet Parks, Avery Architectural and Fine Arts Library, Columbia University, New York, New York; the staff of the Henry Francis Dupont Winterthur Library, Winterthur, Delaware; Mark Weimer, of the George Arents Research Library for Special Collections, Syracuse University, Syracuse, New York, and Barbara Opar, Architectural Librarian, Bird Library of that same institution; Douglas A. Bakken, Director, Archives and Research Library, The Edison Institute, Henry Ford Museum and Greenfield Village, Dearborn, Michigan; Gerald Parsons, Local History and Genealogy Collection, Onondaga

County Public Library, Syracuse, New York; and Katherine Kinsky, Binghamton Public Library, Binghamton, New York. My thanks also to Leila Mattson, Isabel Gulick, and Donald W. Bates.

A number of historians have graciously supplied information for this study. They are: Jean N. Berry, Chair, Historical Commission, Wellesley, Massachusetts; Marion G. Carmier, Curator, Ossining Historical Society, Ossining, New York; Perry G. Fisher, Executive Director, Columbia Historical Association, Washington, D.C.; Marjory Allen Perez, Wayne County Historian, Lyons, New York; Elsie Rufleth, Waterbury Action to Conserve our Heritage, Waterbury, Connecticut; Ann Smith, Director, Mattatuck Museum, Waterbury, Connecticut; and Richard Wright, Onondaga Historical Association, Syracuse, New York.

I want to thank the following people who helped me a great deal in many different ways: J. Brad Benson, Richard M. Billow, Robert Carlson, David and Beth Cathers, Kathleen Clark, Roger G. Cook, Howard and Fran Davies, Robert Edwards, Jerry and Sylvia Galanti, Tom Giddings, Donald and Myra Glen, F. D. Godfrey Sr., Stephen Gray, Thomas A. Greco, Sally Kinsey, Samuel A. Krasney, Victor and Doris Lamb, Raymond and Anne Lauenstein, C. Gordon Lynn, Jr., Robert Mann, Orin and Elizabeth Martin, James D. Robertson, Norman and Joan Roth, James and Diana Rothchild, Terry Shorter, Geneva Surowick, Vincent Valerio, and Robert Williams.

Three of Gustav Stickley's descendants: his daughter, Barbara Stickley Wiles, and two grandsons, Peter and Ben Wiles, have been generous with their time and their reminiscences. I thank them.

For her efficiency, patience, and goodwill I thank my fine typist, Jane Frost.

Summer 1982   MAS

INTRODUCTION

O UNDERSTAND JUST how Gustav Stickley, a furniture manufacturer in central New York State, became involved in the Arts and Crafts Movement and eventually emerged as one of its most important proponents, we must first see how the Movement began in England and how it expanded to the United States. When Gustav Stickley began to publish his *Craftsman* magazine in 1901, he dedicated the whole of the first issue to William Morris (1834–96). This was surely not a haphazard choice for William Morris was the real father of the Arts and Crafts Movement.[1] Morris was an inspiration to Stickley and countless others as a thinker who wrote vigorously about his principles and put them into practice as a craftsman. Morris disliked the badly designed, machine-produced products coming out of factories in his native England in the mid-nineteenth century and felt that the factory worker was being dehumanized by the industrial system. He was inspired by his friend John Ruskin (1818–1900), that great critic of design and art, and such Pre-Raphaelite painter friends as Edward Burne-Jones (1833–98) and Dante Gabriel Rossetti (1828–82) who looked back to the medieval period as a time when the craftsman produced honestly designed, well-executed products by hand in an atmosphere conducive to the simple life.

When Morris married Jane Burden and commissioned his friend Phillip Webb (1831–1915) to build his Red House at Bexley Heath in 1859, he realized that there was no furniture being made that was appropriate to furnish it. Therefore, Webb designed special pieces which Morris, Burne-Jones, and Rossetti decorated. As a result of the collaborative experience of furnishing the Red House, Morris founded Morris, Marshall, Faulkner and Company in 1861, with Webb and Ford Madox Brown (1821–93) designing furniture and Burne-Jones and Rossetti designing the stained glass which was an early mainstay of the business. Morris designed wallpaper, fabrics, rugs, and tapestries since his forte was pattern design. Morris and his associates produced fine products by hand, but they soon discovered that their beautiful crafts products were too expensive for any but rather wealthy customers. The problem of high costs, never solved, tended to make the products of the Arts and Crafts

Movement available only to the well-to-do; thus an envisioned reform of middle-class taste was never completely successful.

By the mid-1870s, Morris had become disenchanted with an economic system that made his products expensive; he advocated an art for all rather than the wealthy few and a production system based on cooperation rather than competition. His concerns led him to become a socialist in 1883 in hopes of changing the economic and social systems for the good of all. Eventually he was to realize that the machine was necessary for production in order to free the laborer from the more arduous aspects of work, and he even became an advocate of the factory as long as it was in a pleasant, nonpolluted setting. Morris was a utopian socialist until the end of his life, but disagreements with party leaders forced his resignation from the Socialist Democratic Federation and the Socialist League which he had helped to found.

In 1890, Morris founded the Kelmscott Press which was to print books as works of art with Morris-designed typeface, handmade paper, illustrations by Walter Crane (1845–1915) and Burne-Jones, and medievally inspired border designs by Morris.

Morris' influence was pervasive, reaching those who knew him and saw his beautifully crafted products. His influence also extended to a wider public with access to the books and articles he wrote and the lectures he gave throughout his career. His related ideals of honest craftsmanship, improvement of the worker's condition, and utopian socialism inspired young designers in England and elsewhere. Motivated by Morris' example and John Ruskin's short-lived and unsuccessful St. George's Guild of 1871, his admirers established several crafts guilds in the 1880s. The Century Guild, formed by Arthur H. Mackmurdo (1851–1942) and Selyen Image (1849–1930) in 1882, produced furniture, textiles, wallpaper, and metalwork. Many of their products were designed by Mackmurdo, a precursor of Art Nouveau design, but in keeping with the guild idea of cooperative labor, most work was not signed by the individual creator. In 1884, the Century Guild published one issue of *The Hobby Horse,* resuming publication in 1886. By 1888, the Century Guild as such was no longer productive although members continued to work together.

In 1884, William Lethaby (1857–1931) and others from the architectural office of Richard Norman Shaw (1831–1912) joined with other designers to form the Art Workers' Guild which was primarily an organization for discussion of mutually interesting topics rather than a crafts production guild; the

Art Workers' Guild was important as a meeting ground for nearly all the English Arts and Crafts designers of the period. Among its members were Morris, Mackmurdo, Norman Shaw, Walter Crane, C. F. A. Voysey (1857–1941), C. R. Ashbee (1863–1942), Edwin Lutyens (1869–1944), and Lewis Day (1845–1910). Since one serious problem of craftsmen was display of their products to the public, several members of the Art Workers' Guild formed the Arts and Crafts Exhibition Society in 1888. This society held annual exhibitions 1888–90 and thereafter, every three years until World War I. The name of this group, originally the Combined Arts Society, was changed to Arts and Crafts Society at the suggestion of the book designer, T. J. Cobden-Sanderson, thereby giving the Movement its name.

The Guild of Handicraft, founded by C. R. Ashbee in 1888, was much closer to the guild spirit of cooperative efforts in the crafts. Ashbee, a socialist, architect, metalwork and jewelry designer, was so imbued with the guild ideal that in 1902 he established a crafts community at Chipping Campden, a small rural town in Gloucestershire. As an educational and social reformer, he saw the Chipping Campden venture as a chance to put many of his ideas into practice; he provided classes in cooking, gardening, citizenship, and swimming and invited his Arts and Crafts friends to lecture there. Unfortunately the Chipping Campden experiment was failing by 1904, and the Guild of Handicraft was dissolved in 1907; Ashbee and his wife continued to live at Chipping Campden until 1911.

Ashbee was one of the major links between the English Arts and Crafts Movement and sympathetic American craftsmen. He first visited the United States in 1896, returning 1900–1901, 1908–1909, and 1915–16. In 1896, he lectured at Cornell University in Ithaca, New York, among many other places and while in Chicago, met Frank Lloyd Wright who became a lifelong friend. While he was lecturing in Buffalo in 1900, his wife went to nearby East Aurora, New York, to meet Elbert Hubbard, who had established his own Roycroft crafts community there. Hubbard later visited the Ashbees in Chipping Campden. In 1909, Ashbee went all the way across the country to California, where he met Charles Sumner Greene whose work he greatly admired. Ashbee lectured in many parts of the United States, presumably disseminating Arts and Crafts ideas as well as promoting the British National Trust, an organization committed to saving historic buildings.[2]

Aside from Ashbee's several American tours, there were other English Arts and Crafts links to the United States in the late 1890s. Magazines were probably most important. The English publication *Studio,* begun in 1893, and its American counterpart, *International Studio,* begun in 1897, contained well-illustrated articles on the Arts and Crafts Exhibition Society exhibits as well as information about the latest designs of various English craftsmen. *The House Beautiful,* begun in Chicago in 1896, was an important source of information on English and American crafts and architecture.

The magazines featuring Arts and Crafts articles must have found an eager readership among members of the Arts and Crafts clubs springing up in the United States during the 1890s. The Boston Society of Arts and Crafts, organized in June 1897, held the first American Arts and Crafts exhibition in 1898; Gustav Stickley was a member of this organization by 1906 and possibly earlier.[3] The Chicago Arts and Crafts Society, founded in October 1897, had many architects as members, among them Frank Lloyd Wright, Myron Hunt, Dwight Perkins, and Robert Spencer. Other related groups included the Minneapolis Arts and Crafts Society (1899, formerly Chalk and Chisel, 1895), the Minneapolis-based Handicraft Guild (1902), and the Society of Arts and Crafts in Grand Rapids (1902).

Not to be outdone by the English, several American groups also formed Arts and Crafts communities. Elbert Hubbard (1856–1915), already mentioned in connection with Ashbee, visited William Morris' Kelmscott Press in 1894. He returned home so impressed that in 1895 he founded the Roycroft Shops in East Aurora, New York, to print handmade books. Eventually he was to publish the monthly *Philistine* which included his most famous work, "Message to Garcia," in 1899. He also published periodic *Little Journies,* biographical studies of famous people. The Roycrofters made a variety of hand-hammered copper products and in 1896 began to build a small quantity of simple, rectilinear furniture inspired to a certain extent by Mackmurdo. The flamboyant, self-styled "Fra" went down on the *Titanic,* but his Roycroft Shops continued to operate until 1938.[4]

Rose Valley, a more idealistically inspired utopian crafts community, was established in Moylan, Pennsylvania, near Philadelphia in 1901. Its founders, architect William P. Price (1861–1916) and Hawley McLanahan, supposedly based their ideal community on the socialist principles of William Morris' *News from Nowhere.* The craftsmen of Rose Valley produced ceramics and furniture until the community went bankrupt in 1909. Between 1903 and 1907, the craftsmen published *The Artsman,* a magazine devoted to the Arts and Crafts. In 1902, Ralf Ratcliffe Whitehead, a great admirer of John Ruskin, started another crafts community, Byrdcliffe, in Woodstock, New York. Byrdcliffe craftsmen produced ceramics and woven goods until their community also failed. American crafts communities were no more successful in the long run than Ashbee's Chipping Campden experiment. There are various reasons for their individual failures, but all seem to have encountered the same problem Morris had faced in his firm, the high cost of handcrafted products not competitive in a free market society.

In central New York where Gustav Stickley was to establish his Craftsman furniture plant and publish his *Craftsman* magazine, there was a lively interest in the Arts and Crafts Movement in the 1890s and early twentieth century. To the west in East Aurora, Hubbard was promoting his Roycroft products, while in Buffalo, Charles Rohlfs (1853–1936) had a small furniture workshop begun in 1890. Adelaide Alsop Robincau (1865–1929), a very talented ceramicist, began publishing *Keramic Studio* in Syracuse in December 1900, and moved to Syracuse in 1901.[5] Although the Robineau house and studio were not designed by Craftsman architects, the light fixtures in her house as well as some of the furniture were Craftsman designs. She and Stickley must have been acquainted since they had common crafts interests. Irene Sargent (1852–1932), a Syracuse University professor of aesthetics and romance languages, was on the scene to provide intellectual stimulation.[6] In Fayetteville, a village near Syracuse, Gustav Stickley's brothers, Leopold (1869–1957) and J. George Stickley established the L. and J. G. Stickley Company in 1902. These brothers, among Gustav Stickley's major competitors, made furniture which resembled his. Harvey Ellis (1852–1904), a Rochester architect, came to work for Gustav Stickley for a brief period 1903–1904. In 1909, a latecomer, Ward Wellington Ward (1875–1932),[7] arrived in Syracuse to design Tudor-inspired houses which were a fine setting for Henry Keck's (1873–1956) stained glass windows and Henry Chapman (1856–1930) Mercer Moravian tiled fireplaces. With all these creative people in the area, upstate New York was a real center for the Arts and Crafts Movement where exciting things were happening.

Gustav Stickley, as we shall see, was to be inspired by many of the ideals of the English Arts and Crafts Movement. To some extent he shared the antiurban, utopian guild spirit of the English. He absorbed a moralistic attitude toward labor and honest craftsmanship from the writings of Ruskin and Morris, and his principles were reinforced by actual contact with English Arts and Crafts leaders and their work. Although he was of the same generation as many of the English craftsmen, he and most of his American contemporaries only entered the Arts and Crafts milieu in the 1890s. By 1900, Stickley was ready to make a name for himself as a leading proponent of the Arts and Crafts Movement in the United States.

Gustav Stickley's career as an important leader of the American Arts and Crafts Movement developed logically, yet it is likely that no one could have foreseen its development or the eventual influence he would exert prior to World War I. Indeed, until Stickley was more than forty years old, his name and his ideas were probably known to very few people. Yet for a brief period, 1900–1916, he designed a new kind of American furniture, promulgated the Arts and Crafts philosophy to an educated and influential segment of the public, and created a domestic architecture in which both his furniture and his philosophy were at home.

GUSTAV STICKLEY
The Craftsman

1

GUSTAV STICKLEY'S EARLY YEARS

AS HAS BEEN THE CASE with many other creative people, Gustav Stickley came from a humble immigrant background. His parents, Leopold and Barbara Schlaeger Stoeckel (later Americanized to Stickley) had come to the United States from Germany. Gustav was born on March 9, 1858, in Osceola, Wisconsin, the eldest child in a large family. At the age of twelve, Gustav (originally spelled Gustave) went to work for his stonemason father, beginning as a mason's tender. He had mastered the work by the age of twelve at which time he received a journeyman's wages.[1] He grew to hate the hard work he had begun so early in life; years later he was to recall those years of stonemasonry vividly:

> It was heavy and tedious labor, much too hard for a boy of my age, and being put to it so early gave me an intense dislike for it. Had I been older and stronger, I might not have realized so keenly its disagreeable features, but as it was, the feeling of the lime and the grinding of the trowel over stone and mortar was especially repugnant to me, and the toil itself meant the utmost physical strain and fatigue.[2]

More than thirty years later when Gustav Stickley was planning houses, he often suggested uncut stone for foundations and chimneys. Rarely was cut stone used!

After a period of excessive drinking and unhappiness, Gustav Stickley's father abandoned the family in the early 1870s. Barbara Stickley, alone with her young children, seems to have moved to nearby Stillwater, Wisconsin, at this point; in 1874 or 1875, the family moved east to live with Mrs. Stickley's brother, Jacob Schlaeger in Laynesboro, Pennsylvania. Gustav Stickley, as eldest son, accepted the responsibility of supporting his large family. He had been forced to leave school after the eighth grade while still in the Midwest because of the family's economic problems. Thus he began his career in the furniture industry with little formal education, his only work skill being stonemasonry.

Jacob Schlaeger owned a small chair factory in nearby Brandt, Pennsylvania, and gave young Gustav a job which provided the young man with his first experience in working with wood, surely an easier medium than hard stone. It was at this time that he came to appreciate wood as a material, an appreciation which he would always retain. In 1906, he reminisced about the Brandt period:

> My first experience in furniture making came when I began work in a small chair factory in the hamlet of Brandt.... where we made the plain wood and cane-seated chairs so much used in those days.... It was the most common-place of stereotyped work, yet from it, I can date my love for working in wood and my appreciation of the beauty and interest to be found in its natural color, texture and grain.[3]

He continued his employment at the Brandt Chair Company until 1884, when he and his two younger brothers, Charles and Albert, moved to Binghamton, New York, a few miles across the state border from Brandt. In Binghamton, the brothers established a wholesale and retail furniture business financed by Schuyler C. Brandt. Their spacious, four-story store sold Grand Rapids black walnut "suits," no doubt ornate in the fashion of the 1880s, in addition to the simpler Brandt chairs and Shaker furniture.

In the mid-1880s, Gustav Stickley married Eda Ann Simmons, daughter of John Simmons of Susquehanna, Pennsylvania. It seems likely that Gustav met his future bride while he was living in Brandt, which was located near Susquehanna. Their courtship was romantic. Eda Ann's mother died and so her father placed her in a convent. Somehow she and Gustav met and began a correspondence, using a milkman to deliver their letters. One September morning, with the help of a milkman, she escaped from the convent to marry Gustav Stickley. Eda Ann Stickley was a gentle, rather retiring woman who did not play an important part in Gustav Stickley's professional life according to Barbara Wiles, Stickley's daughter.

In 1886, the Stickley Brothers Company added a chair factory to their Binghamton enterprise, again with the financial help of Schuyler C. Brandt. It was at this point that Gustav Stickley began to produce the simplified furniture which would later evolve into his distinctive Craftsman products. He explained how this development occurred:

> Before any capital would be put into the concern, it was necessary to show that we were actually manufacturing, and we had no money to buy machinery. I went to a maker of broom handles who had a good turning lathe which he used only part of the time. I hired the use of this and with it blocked out the plainer parts of some very simple chairs made after the "Shaker" model. The rest of them I made by hand, with the aid of a few simple and inexpensive machines which were placed in the loft of the store. All we had was a hand-lathe, boring machine, framing saw and chuck, and the power was transmitted by rope from a neighboring establishment. The wood in shape was dried in the sun on the tin roof of the building. The very primitiveness of this equipment, made necessary by lack of means, furnished what was really a golden opportunity to break away from the monotony of commercial forms, and I turned my attention to reproducing by hand some of the simplest and best models of the Old Colonial, Windsor and other plain chairs, and to a study of this period as a foundation for original work along the same lines.... This was in 1886, and it was the beginning of the "fancy chair" era. The reproduction of the Colonial designs soon became popular, as these "fancy" chairs and rockers proved a most satisfactory substitute for the heavy and commonplace "parlor-suits" of which people were beginning to tire.[4]

An interest in the American past, indeed a Colonial Revival, had started even before the Centennial Exposition held in Philadelphia in 1876. By 1886 when Gustav and his brothers began manufacturing "old Colonial" designs, customers were probably quite receptive to their "fancy chairs." It seems ironic that these chairs were called "fancy" when they were much less ornate than earlier products.

Gustav Stickley's connection with the Stickley Brothers Company was brief. In 1888 or 1889, he formed yet another furniture manufacturing company in Binghamton, leaving the family firm to become the partner of Elgin A. Simonds. Gustav was president of the firm which seems to have had only a short existence in Binghamton.[5] Presumably the Stickley and Simonds Company products were similar to those of Stickley and Brandt, that is, "fancy chairs" inspired by American colonial models or Shaker furniture. Although the Stickley and Simonds Company in Binghamton lasted only two years or so, it was an important association for Gustav; Simonds was to be his partner when he eventually moved to Syracuse, New York.

In 1891, Gustav Stickley's career took a brief but surprising turn. In that year he became vice-president of the new Binghamton Street Railroad which was capitalized at $1.6 million. The electrically powered street railroad or trolley was one of the first of its kind in New York State.[6] Stickley's connection with the street railroad is such a departure from all his earlier businesses that one wonders why and how it happened at all. Perhaps his own Stickley and Simonds Company had not been very profitable during its brief existence and his association with the railroad came about by some fortuitous friendship with the principals in the new corporation; this association lasted only a year or so.

During the years 1892–94, Stickley was Director of Manufacturing Operations at the New York State Prison at Auburn.[7] Using convict labor, Stickley manufactured simple chairs for sale to the public. Stickley's furniture manufacturing experiences in Brandt and Binghamton provided good training for this position. It has been suggested that Stickley designed and made a very special chair during the Auburn years, the electric chair still in place in the prison.[8] His daughter recalled living in Auburn as a child. The Stickleys lived very near the prison and kept a pair of German Shepard dogs as protection against escaped prisoners.

Although occupied with his job at Auburn Prison, Stickley found time to begin a new furniture manufacturing business with his former Binghamton partner, Elgin A. Simonds. In 1892, they purchased property in Eastwood, New York, a suburb of Syracuse, New York, on which to build their new factory. This twenty-eight-lot property was to be the site of the Stickley-Simonds Company and later the home of Stickley's Craftsman workshops. Stickley's first years in Eastwood seem to have been financially insecure. The Panic of 1893, a depression of some magnitude, resulted in many bank and business failures. The recovery was gradual, reaching a turning point only in 1897. This was surely not a good time to start a new business. In fact, three months after Stickley and Simonds had purchased their factory property, a pair of unpaid workers sued for foreclosure of the business.[9] Fortunately the new business was able to continue operations.

For about a year Stickley commuted from Auburn to Syracuse, a distance of some twenty-five miles. In 1893, however, responsibilities of the new business made it necessary for him to move to Syracuse; he lived at the new Yates Hotel as did his partner Simonds. Stickley's family remained in Auburn until 1894 when they moved into a large house at 1001 Walnut Avenue in Syracuse.[10] Only one block away from the Syracuse University campus, their Walnut Avenue home had a prestigious address. The substantial houses in the neighborhood were rather new, most of them constructed in the previous ten years. The houses faced Walnut Park, a block wide green space several blocks long. The fact that Stickley could afford to live in such a good neighborhood while he was developing a new business suggests that the factory was soon successful even during a period of depression and only two years after the threat of foreclosure.

Syracuse was a bustling, growing city in the mid-1890s as its businesses and industries recovered from the 1893 depression. In 1896, its population was 120,124, an increase of 3,560 from the preceding year. The city was served by the Erie Canal and two other canals as well as railroads running in nine directions. Industrial products valued at $72 million were produced that year, and new buildings worth $2,164,410 had been constructed according to the 1896 Syracuse Directory. The financial heart of the city was Clinton Square where the Erie and Oswego canals met. Bank buildings of various styles dominated the square. The Third National Bank, designed by Archimedes Russell in the Richardsonian Romanesque style had been completed in 1886. Across the Erie Canal stood Joseph Lyman Silsbee's Syracuse Savings Bank (1876), an outstanding example of the Venetian Gothic with its brilliant polychromy. Nearby, the Onondaga County Savings Bank (1867) by Horatio Nelson White exemplified the Second Empire style with its mansard roof and clock tower. The Yates Hotel where Stickley had stayed when he first came to Syracuse was two blocks away across the street from the recently built Romanesque Revival City Hall (1894) by Charles E. Colton. These were substantial buildings constructed for the enhancement of the city as well as for its business concerns. Syracuse was also a much larger city than Binghamton; its Eastwood suburb seems to have been a good location for the Stickley-Simonds Company.

In 1896, officers of the Stickley-Simonds Company were listed for the first time in Syracuse directories. Elgin A. Simonds was president and William D. Brewster was listed as manager; Gustav Stickley was treasurer. The same officers were listed through 1899.[11] The chairs produced by Stickley-Simonds were more elaborate than those made by Stickley-Brandt. Their eclectic designs were influenced by Louis XIV, Adam, and Italian Renaissance models; some of the chairs were accurate Chippendale reproductions. *The Decorator and Furnisher* (1895), a trade periodical, noted that "The firm manufactures a large line of artistic and parlour chairs in the English and French styles."[12]

In 1899, Gustav Stickley became involved in an attempt to create an American furniture trust which would absorb all chair manufacturers in the United States. In May, the Stickley-Simonds Company gave an option on its plant to a combine which was to be called the United Chair Manufacturers; the object of the combine was concentration of the entire furniture industry for the sake of efficiency. Later in May, Stickley stated to a local newspaper that the combine, now called the American Chair Company, would be incorporated at $25 million. In July, those interested in the proposed combine met in New York with Charles R. Flint who was a leader in the South American rubber trust but apparently not a furniture manufacturer himself. In August, the proposed chair trust seemed to be a reality and Gustav Stickley was being mentioned as a probable officer. The trust was to be incorporated by October 1. The last Syracuse newspaper article concerning the proposed trust appeared in September 1899; it reported that ninety percent of the American chair companies had agreed to join the trust.[13] At some point in the trust negotiations, Stickley and Simonds severed their business relationship. Gustav Stickley took over the Stickley-Simonds factory, forming the Gustav Stickley Company in 1899. William D. Brewster who had been manager of the Stickley-Simonds Company became Stickley's treasurer and Leopold Stickley, Gustav's brother, became foreman; both positions lasted only one year.[14]

The proposed amalgamation of all American chair companies did not take place. In light of Gustav Stickley's extremely individualistic personality in later years, it seems amazing that he would have even considered such a trust; perhaps the possibility of being an officer of the trust tempted him. His support of such a trust does indicate that he liked to think of business in grandiose terms, a point of view that would later be his downfall. In 1899, he was ready to give up control of his own factory for a role in the larger enterprise. He even severed his partnership with Simonds that year, possibly to promote the trust plan, although he may have desired only to assume complete control of the factory. Simonds went on to establish another furniture company in Syracuse.

Until the end of the 1890s when he made his first trip to Europe, Gustav Stickley was the typical American furniture manufacturer. He had been involved in a number of furniture companies, usually with members of his family. These involvements were usually short lived. There seems to have been a restlessness in his life as he moved from place to place in the northern Pennsylvania-central New York area. Although he had married and produced several children, he never settled long with his family. In 1898, he was forty years old, surely of an age to have found his niche in life. However, at this age he was still searching. By the end of the 1890s, he began to find answers.

2

INFLUENCES FROM EUROPE

I N THE LATE 1890s, Gustav Stickley went to Europe for the first time, visiting England and the Continent. The date of this visit has usually been given as 1898 based on Stickley's own comments concerning the beginnings of his new Craftsman style. Stickley stated that his new furniture designs dated from 1900 and that for a year, presumably prior to 1900 and after his European journey, he had experimented with furniture designs inspired by European Art Nouveau and English Arts and Crafts furniture.[1] In view of the radical changes which began to take place in his furniture designs after this trip, its date is important. While this date cannot be established with certainty, it seems likely that it did occur in 1898. During a period of several months in 1899, he was occupied with the abortive furniture trust plan[2] and thus would have been unable to leave the United States. In 1898, after severing his business relationship with Simonds, and before beginning his own new business, he presumably had free time for European travels.

It is tempting to speculate on what Stickley may have seen in Europe and whom he may have met there. John C. Freeman has written that Stickley met such important English Arts and Crafts figures as T. J. Cobden-Sanderson, William R. Lethaby, Barry Parker, Raymond Unwin, Charles Robert Ashbee, and Charles F. A. Voysey, during a visit to England in 1898, and that he met Samuel Bing and René Lalique in Paris on the same trip.[3] Although articles by or about these men appearing some year later in Stickley's *Craftsman* magazine suggest a Stickley connection with them, there is no evidence that this link was forged in 1898.

Stickley would have gone to Europe with a good idea of what he wanted to experience there. Since childhood he had been an admirer of the work of John Ruskin and William Morris. As a young man in Brandt, Pennsylvania, Gustav had had access to a small library which contained a number of Ruskin's books as well as work by Thomas Carlyle, another popular Victorian reformer whose work he admired.[4] It is not difficult to imagine what particular Ruskinian theories inspired Stickley. Ruskin's *Seven Lamps of Architecture,* first published in 1849, stressed the importance of good craftsmanship and honesty in the use of materials. Ruskin's belief in a world made better by morality in craftsmanship was essentially a reaction against the abuses of the Industrial Revolution in England. In the *Seven Lamps of Architecture* Ruskin discussed the virtues of Gothic architecture, but the comments he made could often apply to furniture as well. In one chapter, "The Lamp of Truth," he categorized "Architectural Deceits" as follows:

> 1st The suggestion of a mode of structure or support, other than the true one; as in pendants of late Gothic roofs.
> 2nd The painting of surfaces to represent some other material than that of which they actually consist (as in the marbling of wood), or the deceptive representation of sculptured ornament upon them.
> 3rd The use of cast or machine-made ornaments of any kind.[5]

For Stickley, increasingly disenchanted with the eclectic, machine-made furniture he had produced during the years in Brandt and Binghamton as well as in his first years in Syracuse, these tenets must have pointed out a new direction toward the honest use of materials.

Ruskin favored handcraft as opposed to machine production, an attitude which Stickley did not share since he had worked for years with machines in furniture production. Still, Ruskin could state his case with fervor as in "The Lamp of Memory," another of the *Seven Lamps*:

> He who would form the creations of his own mind by any other instrument than his own hand, would, also, if he might, give grinding wheels to Heaven's angels, to make their music easier. There is dreaming enough, and earthiness enough, and sensuality enough in human existence without our turning the few glowing moments of it into mechanism; and since our life must at the best be but a vapor that appears for a little time and then vanishes away, let it at least appear as a cloud in the height of Heaven, not as the thick darkness that broods over the blast of the Furnace, and the rolling of the Wheel.[6]

Ruskin's *Stones of Venice* was fully as popular as *Seven Lamps of Architecture*. Published in three volumes between 1851 and 1853, *Stones of*

Venice reiterated ideas found in the earlier book and formed a basis for Arts and Crafts theory. Always concerned with what Peter Collins has called the "philosophical trinity" of Victorian reformers: "the True, the Beautiful and the Good,"[7] Ruskin, the moralist, set down three rules for the design and manufacture of goods:

1. Never encourage the manufacture of any article not absolutely necessary, in the production of which *invention* has no share.
2. Never demand an exact finish for its own sake, but only for some practical or noble end.
3. Never encourage imitation or copying of any kind except for the sake of preserving records of great works.[8]

Another Ruskinian precept which would have appealed to Stickley had to do with the idea that good taste would make men better human beings. Ruskin stated that "What we *like* determines what we *are,* and is the sign of what we are; and to teach taste is inevitably to form character."[9]

William Morris was an early disciple of Ruskin. To Morris "Of the Nature of Gothic" in *Stones of Venice* was "a new gospel and fixed creed."[10] Moreover, as a designer he followed Ruskin's precepts, valuing honesty of expression and honest use of materials as a means of attaining the morally "Beautiful and Good." Morris' *Hopes and Fears for Art,* a collection of essays first published in 1882, did not concern fine art as its title might suggest but rather the "lesser arts" or crafts and the moral basis for their design and production. In an essay entitled "The Art of the People" he wrote in italics of the necessity for an

> *art which is to be made by the people and for the people, as a happiness to the maker and the user.* These virtues are honesty, and the simplicity of life. To make my meaning clearer I will name the opposing vice of the second of these—luxury to wit.

In the same collection of essays, Morris advocated:

> Simplicity of life, begetting simplicity of taste, that is, a love for sweet and lofty things, is of all matters the most necessary for the birth of

the new and better art we crave for; simplicity everywhere, in the palace as well as in the cottage.[11]

Morris' design philosophy is concisely summed up in two pieces of advice he gave to workmen:

Never forget the material you are working with ... the special limitations of the material should be a pleasure to you, not a hindrance.

And:

Don't copy any style at all, but make your own; yet you must study the history of your art, or you will be nose-led by the first bad copyist of it that you come across.[12]

Gustav Stickley must have been thoroughly imbued with the philosophies of Ruskin and Morris by the late 1890s. Their works were very popular in the United States and widely available. He paid his debt to them by devoting the first two issues of his *Craftsman* magazine to them in 1901. Although his own business practices were not completely based on Ruskin-Morris precepts and his own furniture designs were not copied from those of Morris and Company, the philosophies of these two men were of great importance as a basis of all Stickley was to accomplish. For a designer and furniture manufacturer like Stickley, mere words of design philosophy were not enough, important though they were. Design is a visual exercise, and nothing can take the place of seeing the designed object. Before Stickley went to Europe, he was probably familiar with several European Arts and Crafts periodicals.

He had access to *Studio* and *International Studio,* since both magazines were available in the Syracuse University Library located only a block away from his house, and he apparently subscribed to the German Arts and Crafts periodical, *Deutsche Kunst und Dekoration*[13] published in Darmstadt 1897–1914. He had been familiar with the German language from childhood since his parents spoke German, and thus the language presented no problems to him.

It seems likely that Stickley would have also read *The House Beautiful* from its inception in 1896, although it did not have a large circulation. Thus he would have been aware of recent European design developments as well as Arts and Crafts design philosophy before his trip. Furthermore, he would have gone to Europe armed with the names of designers, groups, and shops he wanted to visit, although his idol, William Morris had died in 1896, and John Ruskin was in no mental condition to receive visitors.

He went to England to see at first hand the English designs which would profoundly affect him. What might this knowledgeable visitor have seen? Perhaps one of the first spots on his itinerary would have been the South Kensington Museum where Arts and Crafts exhibits were held periodically showing the furniture, metal work, ceramics, and fabrics of the best English designers.[14] There he could also see the Green Dining room, a complete interior largely designed by Phillip Webb and executed by William Morris' firm in 1866. Although no longer new by the 1890s, the Green Dining Room would have seemed impressive to Stickley as an example of a total environment, not just an exhibition space with isolated pieces on display.

Stickley may have had a hard time finding London retail shops in which Arts and Crafts furniture was displayed. Hermann Muthesius noted a few years later that there was "almost a total absence of shops devoted to the handicrafts in the way that certain firms in Berlin and Paris are."[15] It seems likely that Stickley sought out the premises of Morris and Company which William Morris had organized in 1861 as Morris, Marshall, Faulkner and Company. Although Morris had died in 1896, his firm continued to operate. At Morris and Company Stickley may have seen a Morris chair, comfortable because its back could be moved into several positions; Gustav would later produce several Craftsman versions of the Morris chair. In addition to heavy cabinet pieces and chairs he may have seen the lighter weight chairs and tables which the firm produced. Although Morris had advocated good design for every man, the beautifully designed and executed produces his firm sold tended to be too expensive for the average pocketbook.

Stickley may have visited the Heal and Son store to see less expensive furniture. Heal's specialized in bedroom furniture, usually of traditional design. However, Ambrose Heal, Jr., influenced by Voysey, Lethaby, and Ashbee, had introduced a simple oak bedroom suite of his own design in 1897.[16] Thus Stickley could have seen examples of relatively inexpensive Arts and Crafts furniture at Heal's as well as Morris and Company's expensive handcrafted furniture.

Another shop where Stickley could have seen Arts and Crafts furniture was Liberty and Company on Regent Street. Founded in 1875 by Arthur Lazenby Liberty (1843–1917), the store originally specialized in oriental fabrics, blue and white china, and other goods which appealed to aesthetes of the period, Whistler and Rossetti among others. Soon furniture and decorative items were added to the stock. Leonard Wyburd designed rectilinear inlaid oak and mahogany furniture for Liberty, while furniture designed by George Walton reflected the influence of Morris and Voysey. Liberty imported Art Nouveau items from Europe during the 1890s, eventually evolving such an individualized stock that the Art Nouveau style was even called "Stile Liberty" in Italy. In keeping with the Arts and Crafts ideal of the environment designed well in all its aspects, Liberty and Company even had a women's clothing department to sell dresses in harmony with Liberty interiors. Liberty and Company made good design commercially successful by rejecting the Arts and Crafts ideal of individual hand craftsmanship and combining handicraft with machine production.[17]

Stickley may have also seen examples of Voysey's work. In 1898, Stickley would have been too late upon the London scene to visit Mackmurdo's Century Guild which had disbanded a decade earlier.[18] However, he may have sought out Mackmurdo's furniture. A Mackmurdo desk (plate 1), designed c. 1886 for the Century Guild and pictured in *Studio* in 1899, may have inspired Stickley. Its sturdy, unornamented design and oak wood were emulated in Craftsman furniture, although the rounded feet and tapered legs were not.

Voysey, like so many other Arts and Crafts designers, had been trained as an architect; however, in common with other leaders of the Movement, he designed in many media such as wallpaper, fabrics, metal, and furniture. A lady's work cabinet (plate 2), illustrated in *Studio* in October 1893, might be taken as an example of his simple, elegant furniture of the period. Constructed of oak stained green, the straight lines, slightly tapered legs, strap hinges, and curved apron are typical of his furniture. Often the metal fittings of his furniture were elaborated with flower, leaf, or heart motifs. Although Voysey's furniture was often made of oak, the primary wood Stickley was to use for his Craftsman furniture, both used other woods on occasion.

Although Stickley was not lucky enough to be in London for one of the Arts and Crafts Exhibition Society shows, he could have read about the 1896 exhibit in *Studio*. It was at the 1896 Arts and Crafts Exhibition that work by the talented Scotch architect and designer Charles Rennie Mackintosh

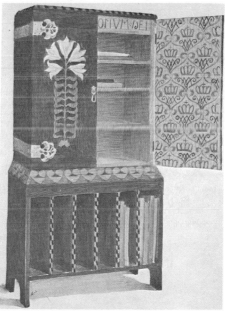

1. Writing table, Arthur H. Mackmurdo, c. 1886. *Studio* 16 (1899): 187.

2. Lady's work cabinet, C. F. A. Voysey, c. 1893. *Studio* 2 (1893): 12.

3. Linen press, Charles R. Mackintosh, c. 1896. *Studio* 11 (1897): 96.

4. Music cabinet, M. H. Baillie Scott, 1895. *International Studio* 5 (1898): following 94.

(1868–1928) was first presented to the English public who greeted it with mixed opinions; however, a two-part article on Mackintosh and his Glasgow circle appeared in *Studio* in June and September 1897, as a result of the Society exhibit. Stickley may have seen Mackintosh's boxy, inlaid linen press (plate 3) in the periodical. Since Mackintosh's activities were centered in Glasgow where he was designing a chain of tea rooms for the Misses Cranston between 1896 and 1916, Stickley would have had to go to Scotland to see Mackintosh's Art Nouveau furniture. There is no evidence that he did; Art Nouveau was to hold little appeal for him.

Stickley may have seen furniture and metalwork being produced by Ashbee's Guild of Handicraft to the design of Mackay Hugh Baillie Scott (1865–1945) for Ernst Ludwig, Grand Duke of Hesse. Baillie Scott's important commission for the redecorating of the Drawing Room and Dining Room of the Ducal Palace in Darmstadt, Germany, was begun in 1897, but the furniture was not completed until 1898.[19] It is not hard to imagine that Stickley would have visited the premises of the Guild of Handicraft, hoping to see this furniture that he had read about in *Studio* and *International Studio* in 1898. The music cabinet (plate 4) with its clean lines and simplicity of design would have appealed to Stickley although he might not have admired the colorful flowers with which it was decorated. As a designer of furniture and houses Baillie Scott was to have a significant influence on Stickley eventually.

Stickley probably visited the Guild of Handicraft retail shop at 16a Brook Street which Ashbee had opened in 1890. It is possible that Stickley had already met Ashbee two years earlier in 1896, when the Englishman was touring the eastern United States.[20] The Ashbee influence was at least as much philosophical as design oriented. The idea of the totally designed interior, suggested by William Morris' work as early as the 1860s, was reinforced by Ashbee and others. Originally trained as an architect, Ashbee designed his Chelsea house, "Magpie and Stump," and everything in it with the help of his Guild friends. It is tempting to think that Gustav Stickley might have been invited to visit this house, designed in 1895 and illustrated in *Studio* and *Dekorative Kunst.*[21]

In the realm of architecture the two Arts and Crafts designers whose work had some influence on Stickley's Craftsman houses were Baillie Scott and Voysey, who had a common interest in the design of the relatively small country house. Both were inspired by English vernacular architecture as a basis for their "free" style, an attempt to break away from the architectural historicism so common in the late nineteenth century. Both architects were interested in the idea of the totally designed interior environment, a preoccupation of the English Arts and Crafts guilds. It was details of their work rather than floor plans and elevations which appealed to Stickley. Such details as grouped, small-paned casement windows, prominent, steeply sloping rooflines, doors with heavy hand wrought hinges and hardware, half-timbering and built-in furniture would later be emulated in the Craftsman house. Voysey and Baillie Scott floor plans, usually asymmetrical with wings or bays extending outward from the core of the house, did not have any substantial influence on the Craftsman house, possibly because Stickley houses were usually designed for small suburban sites rather than the country acres where there was room for spreading wings or traditional English courtyards.

There is no evidence that Stickley had any particular interest in architecture in 1898. He was, after all, a furniture manufacturer, not an architect. While he could have admired Voysey and Baillie Scott houses along with their furniture in *Studio,* he may not have been familiar with such periodicals as *Builder, British Architect,* and *Building News* where a number of their houses were featured during the 1890s. He may not have had access to their rural houses buried deep in the English countryside, but he could have easily gone to Bedford Park in London to see suburban houses.

Bedford Park, a garden suburb on the western edge of London, was planned as a middle class housing area in the 1870s. Richard Norman Shaw, the well-known Queen Anne architect, was Estate Architect to Bedford Park beginning in 1877. He planned a number of small single, semidetached and terrace houses for the area's winding streets. Soon these inexpensive houses became popular with leaders of the arts. Muthesius described Bedford Park as "the refuge of the aesthetes" and commented that "soon Bedford Park actually became a sight which no American passing through London could miss seeing."[22] Although Norman Shaw's unpretentious two-story houses were no longer new when Stickley went to London, he may have found them attractive.

Stickley may have been interested in seeing Voysey's J. W. Forster house (plate 5) in Bedford Park which had been published in the *British Architect* in 1891. Planned for a very narrow site, the tall Forster house had a side entrance and only a parlor, kitchen and service rooms on the ground floor. This was the small house type Stickley would later develop in the United States, convenient and relatively inexpensive. Except for exterior details, the front elevation of the house has little real resemblance to the American Craftsman house.

5. J. M. Forster house, Bedford Park, London, C. F. A. Voysey, c. 1891. *British Architect* (September 18, 1891).

We can imagine Stickley's days in England as a tourist with a serious purpose: to see the furniture and buildings he had only known in periodical articles before this trip. The ideals of Ruskin and Morris which he had been absorbing for years were given visible form in the various places he could have visited in and near London. He could see furniture by Morris and Company, Heal and Son, Liberty and Company, Mackmurdo, Voysey, and Baillie Scott. The ideal of the integrated interior would have been reinforced through English example. The design of the small house of "free" style would have appealed to him.

During this 1898 trip, Stickley probably visited the Continent where Art Nouveau was indeed the new art. Although Stickley went to France, Austria, and Germany to see examples of Art Nouveau, there was little Art Nouveau influence on his work after he returned home. However, the number of articles on Art Nouveau in general and French Art Nouveau in particular in early volumes of *The Craftsman*[23] indicates that Stickley had a more than casual interest in the style.

It seems likely that one of the first places that Stickley visited in France was the Paris shop of Samuel Bing. It was the name of Bing's store, the Salon de l'art nouveau, that gave the pervasive movement its name. Like Liberty in London, Bing had begun his mercantile career as a dealer in oriental art. His goods were so popular that he opened a branch in New York, where John LaFarge and Louis Comfort Tiffany were among his best customers.[24] Possibly Stickley visited the New York store before going to Europe since he collected Japanese prints and admired oriental design.[25]

Bing, like Liberty, became interested in new art forms during the 1890s. With the aid of Frank Brangwyn, an English painter earlier associated with William Morris, and Louis Bonnier, a French architect, Bing transformed his store into a showcase for Art Nouveau. The newly renovated store opened on December 26, 1895, with works by such "modern" artists as Beardsley, Signac, Denis, Khnopff, Pissaro, Sérusier, Toulouse-Lautrec, Vuillard, and Whistler. The salon also included glass by Tiffany and Gallé, Lalique jewelry, and two rooms with furniture designed by Van der Velde.[26]

Like William Morris and other English Arts and Crafts designers, the Belgian architect, Henry Van der Velde (1863–1957) was a master of many media. He designed graphics, wallpaper, fabrics, carpets, furniture, metalwork, ceramics, and even women's dresses, thus sharing in the English Arts and Crafts ideal of the total environment. Stickley would have admired the structural articulation of Van der Velde's furniture for in 1898 the Belgian designer was still under the influence of English design and had not yet created the asymmetrical, biomorphic, curved furniture he would later design.

Even though sinuously curved French Art Nouveau designs were quite different from English Arts and Crafts counterparts, there was a great interest in English design in France during the 1890s. Art Nouveau was even called the "Yachting Style" on occasion, yachts being considered English. In 1898, Samuel Bing expressed his appreciation of the English Arts and Crafts Movement or perhaps the related Aesthetic Movement when he wrote, "When English creations began to appear, a cry of delight sounded throughout Europe. Its echo can still be heard in every corner."[27] Thus Stickley would have found an attitude toward total design at the Salon de l'art nouveau which reflected that in England even if the expression of attitude was different.

Gustav Stickley's European journey served to reinforce his developing design philosophy which was based on Ruskin and Morris. His travels were valuable in that he had the chance to see what was being produced rather than simply reading about new designs. He may have met the men responsible for those new designs, establishing personal contacts which would be useful to him in the future. The European experience was of vital importance to him; in a design sense, it literally transformed him.

He came home to Syracuse, New York, inspired. He started his own furniture manufacturing company in 1899. He later wrote a short account of this period:

> In 1900 I stopped using the standard patterns and finishes, and began to make all kinds of furniture after my own designs, independently of what other people were doing, or of any necessity to fit my designs, woods and finishes to any other factory. For about a year I experimented with more or less fantastic forms.... My frequent journeys to Europe... interested me much in the decorative use of plant forms, and I followed the suggestion.... After experimenting with a number of pieces, such as small tables giving in their form a conventionalized suggestion of such plants as the mallow, the sunflower and the pansey, I abandoned the idea.... Conventionalized plant-forms are beautiful and fitting when used solely for dcoration, but anyone who starts to make a piece of furniture with a decorative form in mind, starts at the wrong end. The sole consideration at the basis of design must be the thing itself and not its ornamentation.

The Arts and Crafts movement was more nearly in harmony with what I had in mind, but even that did not involve a return to the sturdy and primitive forms that were meant for usefulness alone, and I began to work along the lines of a direct application of the fundamental principles of structure to the designing and craftsmanship of my furniture.[28]

After Stickley rejected the plant forms of Art Nouveau, he created his distinctive Craftsman furniture based on structural principles. Those "sturdy and primitive forms" were among Gustav Stickley's important contributions to American design.

3

THE BEGINNINGS OF THE CRAFTSMAN EMPIRE

OR GUSTAV STICKLEY the final years of the nineteenth century and the beginning of the twentieth century must have been cataclysmic. He had recently returned from Europe where he had seen at first hand the Arts and Crafts furniture which was so different from what he had been producing for over twenty years; indeed, English Arts and Crafts furniture had no real counterpart in the entire United States with the possible exception of Roycroft furniture.[1] He became involved with the abortive attempt to unite all American furniture manufacturers in one gigantic trust. He and his partner, Elgin A. Simonds severed their business connection and Gustav established his own company. In 1898, while he was still involved with the Stickley-Simonds partnership, he began the design experiments which eventually were to lead to his own distinctive Craftsman furniture. What a lively and hectic time it must have been! He was later to write that:

> The first pieces of Craftsman furniture were completed in 1898 and then for two years I worked steadily over the development of forms, the adjustment of proportions and the search for a finish which would protect the wood and mellow it in color without sacrificing its natural woody quality.[2]

The experimental designs were inspired by the English Arts and Crafts and European Art Nouveau furniture he had seen and read about in *Studio* and *International Studio*. Since he had been involved primarily with chair manufacture in the past, his first experimental designs were also chairs; however, he soon extended his range to include benches, tables, desks, and sideboards. In July 1900, he exhibited his radically new designs at the semiannual furniture trade show in Grand Rapids, Michigan, announcing his arrival on the scene in the trade publication *American Cabinet Maker and Upholsterer*:

> The Gustave Stickley Company will show a beautiful line of diners and rockers at Grand Rapids. They will be represented by Lee [Leopold] Stickley.... Mr. [Gustave] Stickley has devoted much of his time to the new finish called Austrian Oak, and has succeeded in turning out some handsome designs that cannot fail to impress the buyers of fine goods favorably. The line will contain a shade of green, greatly resembling gun metal.[3]

In October 1900, a *House Beautiful* article entitled "Some Sensible Furniture" extolled Stickley's furniture and pictured five pieces although Stickley was not credited with their design and manufacture.[4] His Poppy table and Celandine tabourette were compared with furniture forms of the Glasgow school, that is, designs by Charles Rennie Mackintosh and his circle in Scotland. However, the furniture singled out for praise was the heavier pieces described as "severely plain." Their solidity, "medieval quality," and finish in weathered oak, gun-metal gray, and Tyrolian green were admired. It is significant that Stickley's new furniture was the subject of editorial notice as soon as it was introduced to the public. Furthermore, this *House Beautiful* article introduced the furniture to exactly that segment of the public which would be interested in buying it.

Stickley's Grand Rapids furniture exhibit apparently impressed principals of the Chicago based Tobey Furniture Company who began marketing it later in 1900 with extensive advertising. It was called the "New" furniture and marked with the Tobey label; Gustav Stickley was not mentioned in their advertisements. A double-page Tobey advertisement in the December 1900 *House Beautiful,* certainly designed to appeal to the Christmas shopper, illustrated a number of Stickley's designs which were described as "angular, plain and severe";[5] his Tyrolian green and gun-metal gray wax finishes, perhaps inspired by Voysey (plate 2), were pointed out as innovations.

Stickley's association with the Tobey Furniture Company was short lived, probably because he was an extremely independent man who did not like working arrangements with other people. In late 1900, he rented part of the lavish Crouse Stables (plate 6) to use as showroom and office space which he now needed as an independent furniture manufacturer and retailer.[6] Although today we may consider a stable as strictly utilitarian architecture, such was not the case in the late nineteenth century. The Crouse Stables, located at 207 South State Street in Syracuse, had been built in 1887–88 to the design of

6. Crouse Stables, Syracuse, New York, 1887–88, elevation. George Arents Research Library, Syracuse University.

Archimedes Russell, a noted local architect, for D. Edgar Crouse, a wealthy man about town. The $200,000 Queen Anne structure contained elegant bachelor quarters decorated by Herter Brothers of New York for the owner and brass-trimmed porcelain feed bowls for the horses.[7] The prominent location of the Crouse Stables, facing Fayette Park along with expensive houses owned by the upper crust of Syracuse, made the picturesquely asymmetrical stables an important local building. The Herter interior featured paneling of rosewood and mahogany and a generally oriental scheme of decoration with Persian rugs, Bengal tiger skins, and Chinese ceramics. When Stickley established his headquarters there the stables had been used for several years as a clubhouse for the Syracuse Athletic Association, presumably requiring alterations for new functions. It is difficult to imagine Stickley's austere furniture in a sumptuous Herter Brothers setting; he made alterations by 1903, and perhaps as soon as he moved in.[8] Although Stickley was to call the Crouse Stables the Craftsman Building, he never owned the structure.[9] Since he shared it with several other businesses,[10] his showrooms were probably not extensive although it was a large structure. He did have enough room to accommodate his expanding activities; in 1901, offices of his new *Craftsman* magazine would be located there and in 1903 he would use the Crouse Stables for an Arts and Crafts exhibition.[11] He also sponsored periodic Arts and Crafts lectures there to educate the public. The local prominence of the Crouse Stables provided a certain status for Stickley's United Crafts or Craftsman enterprises as he presented his products to the public. Moreover, since he now had his own showrooms and would soon begin to publish his own catalogs, he had no need of affiliation with any other company. Thus the Crouse Stables provided a firm base of operations for Stickley during the early years of the century until 1905, when he moved his operations to New York.

Some of the Craftsman furniture Stickley exhibited in his new Syracuse headquarters in 1900 was probably identical to the pieces which had been sold so briefly by the Tobey Company. His first catalog illustrated several delicately proportioned tea tables (plate 7) inspired by Art Nouveau designs; the prominently keyed tenon used in the Celandine and Pansy tables was a detail he also used in more massive designs such as the bungalow library table (plate 8).[12] Tipped in on the same page as the heavy bungalow library table, the delicate, rush-seated bungalow armchair has a curved apron and curved back slats. Soon, the lightweight bungalow armchair was replaced by such pieces as his uncompromisingly rectilinear Eastwood armchair (plate 9), named for his Eastwood factory and designed c. 1901, has uncompromisingly straight lines. Stickley must have had a special fondness for this chair since he continued to produce it for at least twelve years.[13]

It is difficult to ascertain just how much of the production of this early furniture, or indeed any of Stickley's furniture, was a machine process and how much was the type of handicraft advocated by Ruskin, Morris, and other English Arts and Crafts leaders. David Cathers has pointed out the differences in measurements in several examples of a single Stickley design,[14] an indication that the individual worker may have had a good deal of freedom in the construction of a single piece rather than being part of an assembly line. According to his grandson, Gustav Stickley's design process may explain discrepancies in furniture measurements. Gustav would explain the design concept to his workman verbally, waving his hands to indicate the general shape and features of the piece. Then the workman would build the piece and show it to Stickley who would inspect it, again indicating changes by waving his hands. Another model would be built incorporating the changes. This process continued until Stickley approved of the design which then went into production. Only at this point would measured drawings be made. Although Stickley was fully able to use all the tools and machinery employed by his workmen, he preferred this method of design to doing measured drawings himself.[15]

It may well be that Stickley was inspired by one or several American manufacturers when he began to design his early oak furniture. George F. Clingman, the manager of the Tobey Furniture Company, disputed Stickley's later claims of originality in design on several grounds. First, Clingman claimed that in 1885 he had designed the "first simple plain piece of mission furniture," an armchair, for John A. Colby and Sons. Second, Clingman claimed that the Tobey Furniture Company was producing a mission chair and related pieces during the spring of 1900, before the furniture show in Grand Rapids; he cited an article published on April 29, 1900, in a Chicago newspaper as evidence. Third, Clingman claimed that he had given Gustav Stickley the ideas for his early rectilinear designs when they met during the Grand Rapids furniture show; furthermore, he claimed that he had even made sketches for Stickley of "several large sofas with square posts and flat arms with loose pillow seats and backs; some broad arm rockers and chairs, several styles of tables and one or two screens" and encouraged Stickley to add such pieces to his line.[16]

Gustav Stickley always insisted upon calling his furniture "Craftsman" although it has been referred to in a more general way as "mission" or "mission oak." To call his furniture "mission" is to misunderstand Stickley's aspirations and the influences upon him. The furniture used in the old California missions supposedly inspired a New York furniture manufacturer, Joseph P. McHugh, who made some much publicized, straight-lined oak furniture in 1900. McHugh claimed that he had originated mission oak, and he does seem to be

27

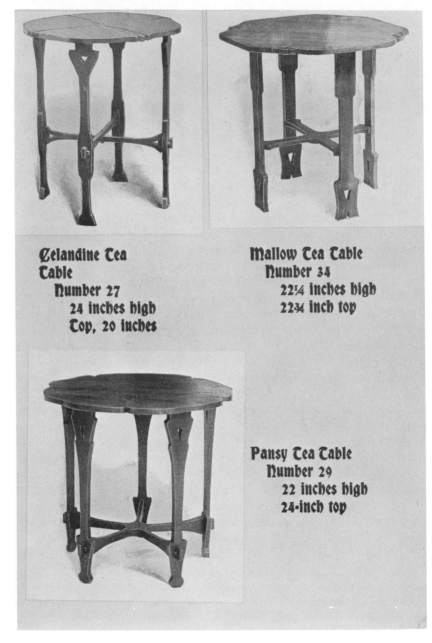

Celandine Tea Table
Number 27
24 inches high
Top, 20 inches

Mallow Tea Table
Number 34
22¼ inches high
22¾ inch top

Pansy Tea Table
Number 29
22 inches high
24-inch top

7, 8. *New Furniture from the Workshop of Gustav Stickley Cabinet Maker Syracuse NY USA*

Bungalow
Library
Table
 Top, 30 x 48 in.
  Number 404

Bungalow
Arm
Chair
 Rush
 Seat
  Number
  1289A

No. I. c. 1900.

9. Eastwood armchair, Gustav Stickley, c. 1901. Photograph courtesy of Jordan Volpe Gallery, New York, New York.

the first person to use the term.[17] His designs were rather crude, however, and it was Gustav Stickley who was to achieve the greater success with his generically "mission" furniture. If any generic name were necessary for Stickley's furniture, it would more appropriately be "Arts and Crafts" since he was more generally inspired by the ideals of the English Arts and Crafts Movement.

Stickley must have chosen the Craftsman name for his company and its products after considerable thought. It was a fitting name which reflected several of his concerns. First, his furniture, unlike most mass-produced, machine-made pieces of the time, was crafted by men trained in hand methods of production. This is not to say that his workers made the furniture entirely by hand. They certainly used machines, but their products were carefully made and the finishes of which Stickley was so proud were applied by hand. Thus Craftsman furniture was the result of a combination of machine and hand methods. Second, the word "Craftsman" reflects Stickley's interest in the medieval guild system of production in which there was a master craftsman working for the common good with other members of the guild. Inspired by the pervasive guild spirit of the English Arts and Crafts Movement,[18] Stickley even ran his company as a modified guild for a few years from 1901 to 1904. He called his guild the United Crafts; according to the Syracuse *Post Standard* (September 15, 1901), its aim was:

> the raising of the general intelligence of the worker, by the increase of his leisure and the multiplication of his means of pleasure and culture, the endeavor to substitute the luxury of taste for the luxury of costliness, and to do something along the Morris idea that all men shall have work to do which shall be worth doing, and be pleased to do it.

Although his workers were paid wages, they also participated in profit-sharing. The Syracuse *Post Standard* (January 6, 1902) noted that Stickley had celebrated New Years Day 1901, by distributing $2,000 in gold coins to his seventy workers as dividends. The United Crafts profit-sharing guild system was to become unsuccessful financially by 1904, when it was discontinued. Also, his work force had grown to two hundred by then according to his pamphlet "What Is Wrought in the Craftsman Workshops," and the working intimacy of a crafts guild was probably no longer possible.

In addition to the Craftsman designation for his company, Stickley adopted a medieval joiner's compass with the motto, "Als ik kan" (plate 10), as his distinctive symbol in 1901. This symbolic use of a medieval hand tool is yet another reflection of Stickley's interest in the middle ages when the craftsman made his products by hand. The "Als ik kan" motto, roughly translated from Flemish as "As I can" or more broadly as "The best that I can," comes from the Flemish painter Jan van Eyck via William Morris, who had used the motto in his house at Bexley Heath. Apparently Stickley was very fond of this symbol; he used it in various forms as a shopmark on his furniture and as a signature on drawings throughout his career. He even registered it as a trademark, along with his "Craftsman" name. It is difficult to imagine a more appropriate symbol for Stickley, incorporating as it does a tribute to Morris and to the medieval craftsman. His motto is a promise of the highest possible quality for all the products he produced.

31

10. Joiner's compass with Stickley motto, c. 1901.

Stickley must have been very busy during 1901. Having discontinued the production of most of the furniture developed for sale by Tobey in favor of his plainer, straight-lined furniture such as the Eastwood chair, he was now developing his own Craftsman style. For this new furniture he had picked the perfect name, "Craftsman," and his distinctive shopmark which beautifully expressed his commitment to the Arts and Crafts idea of quality execution and reflected the Arts and Crafts interest in medievalism. He had converted part of the prominently located Crouse Stables for use as an appropriate showroom and office space. Although designing, producing, and selling this new and different furniture would have been a full-time job for most men, Gustav Stickley somehow found the time and energy in 1901 to start an important new venture for which he had no training at all. That new venture was *The Craftsman* magazine which he began publishing in October of that momentous year.

The Craftsman was to become the leading voice of the Arts and Crafts Movement in the United States. In its pages Stickley had the opportunity to explore the diverse subjects which interested him, sometimes writing about them himself, sometimes having others write articles for him. His magazine always reflected his concerns; thus *The Craftsman* is a good guide to his beliefs and enthusiasms. Those enthusiasms included varied subjects from handicrafts, as might be expected, to mushroom culture, not necessarily to be expected. In the area of crafts, for example, there were articles on the American Van Briggle, Rockwood, Merrimac, and Chelsea ceramics studios; French jewelry designer René Lalique; and English bookbinder T. J. Cobden-Sanderson. Although literature was never a major component of *The Craftsman,* one could read works by Tolstoy and Gorkey in its pages and poetry by Robert Frost, Carl Sandburg, and Amy Lowell.[19]

Stickley's reasons for publishing *The Craftsman* were twofold. First, he sincerely wanted to publicize the ideas of the English Arts and Crafts Movement and related American trends. Second, he wished to publicize his own Craftsman furniture which appeared prominently in every issue. In 1904, he stated his goal for the magazine on the occasion of its third anniversary:

> At the beginning, my purpose was to publish any writing which might increase public respect for honest intelligent labor; advance the cause of civic improvement; diffuse a critical knowledge of modern art, as shown in its most characteristic examples chosen from the

33

fine, decorative, or industrial divisions; advocate the "intergal education," or in other words, the simultaneous training of hand and brain;
and thus help to make the workshop an adjunct of the school.

Throughout the existence of *The Craftsman* I have sought
with great zeal, unflinching purpose and perfect modesty, to benefit
the people.[20]

As the years passed until the magazine went out of existence in 1916, Stickley
was to publish articles on such diverse topics as socialism, manual arts training, gardens, Japan, and American Indians. As he became increasingly interested in a perfect setting for his craftsman furniture, house design emerged
as a prominent feature of Stickley's magazine. He did not neglect the accomplishments of architects and planners, including many articles about or by
prominent practitioners of the period.

During the formative period of *The Craftsman,* Stickley had the good
fortune to have as his associate Syracuse University professor Irene Sargent.
Dr. Sargent is said to have studied at Harvard with art historian Charles Eliot
Norton and to have been associated with Bernard Berensen in Italy, although
no evidence of these connections exists. She taught French and Italian, later
adding aesthetics and art history to her repertoire. In 1926, she became the
second woman to receive honorary membership in the American Institute of
Architects for her contributions to the profession as a teacher of architectural
history. She wrote twenty-six of the thirty-three articles published in *The
Craftsman* between October 1901 and March 1902; by 1905, when she
discontinued her contributions, she had written a total of eighty-four
Craftsman articles.[21]

In view of her extensive contribution to *The Craftsman,* one might
conclude that it was her magazine and indeed her part in its formulation was
great. Gustav Stickley had never before written for publication and he was
occupied with the design and production of furniture when he began *The
Craftsman.* He must have been delighted to have the well-qualified Dr. Sargent
as primary contributor during those early years. Although no one knows
whose idea *The Craftsman* was, it may well have been Irene Sargent's rather
than Stickley's. Certainly the first few issues have a coherence of theme and
format unlike later issues when other authors began to contribute articles.

The first issue of *The Craftsman* was devoted to William Morris to
whom Stickley owed so much of his design philosophy. The small format

magazine was printed on textured paper with red illumination. The title page of the first issue (plate 11), typical of the early issues, had a medievally inspired typeface and a border design reminiscent of Morris' Kelmscot Press books. Irene Sargent wrote the five Morris articles, and Stickley presumably wrote the three brief unsigned pieces following, one of which was entitled "An Argument for Simplicity in Household Furnishings." A number of glossy illustrations of his United Crafts furniture completed the issue.

The English Arts and Crafts theme established in the first issue was repeated in subsequent months; the second issue was devoted to John Ruskin, the third to medieval craft guilds, and the fourth to textile design. The fifth issue (February 1902) with a focus on Robert Owen, the utopian socialist, and his factory reforms, marks the beginning of real diversification in *The Craftsman*. No longer were the majority of articles in an issue on a single person or theme; rather, Stickley's varied interests found expression in *The Craftsman*. Although the emphasis on various topics waned or increased as Stickley's interests refocused through the years, there was a remarkable coherence of overall concept in *The Craftsman* until the last years when Stickley's Craftsman empire began to fall apart. The topics included in *The Craftsman* should be thought of as pieces of a mosaic which was Stickley's Craftsman philosophy.

Beginning with the first issue, one topic explored in *The Craftsman* was socialism. Irene Sargent's "William Morris, His Socialistic Career" begins with a note from the editor, Stickley, which is almost a warning or apology to the reader:

> In an effort to offer an accurate portrait-sketch of William Morris, the artist-socialist, handicraftsman, poet and man of business, we have thought it best not to conceal those characteristics which separated him so widely from the men of his class and condition. The force and even vehemence of his nature led him to extremes which are inconceivable to the calm-minded and conservative.[22]

Since Stickley used the word "extremes" to describe Morris' socialism, it seems clear that he either was not in complete agreement with Morris' political activities or was fearful of his readers' reactions. His accurate description of Morris as an "artist-socialist" might well be a self-description. Both men had a

The
Craftsman

"The lyf so short
the craft so
long to
lerne"

WILLIAM MORRIS
Some thoughts
upon
His life: work & influence

Published on the first day
of each month by THE
UNITED CRAFTS at
EASTWOOD, NEW YORK

Price 20 cents the copy

11. Cover, *The Craftsman* 1, no. 1 (October 1901).

deep concern for the average working man and hoped to make his life more satisfying. Irene Sargent saw Morris as a socialist who advocated "equality, good-will and kindness" achieved through cooperative action for a better distribution of labor, land, and capital. According to her, "His Socialism from the beginning was of the heart, not of the head." This description could also fit Stickley's socialist leanings. However, Stickley had put his beliefs into practice for a short time when he divided part of his profits with his United Crafts workers.

Articles on socialism continued to be published in *The Craftsman,* especially during its early years. Irene Sargent had a particular interest in the ideas of Prince Peter Alexivich Kropotkin (1842–1921), writing three *Craftsman* articles on his ideas and mentioning him in a fourth. In "A Chapter from Prince Kropotkin's 'Mutual Aid in the Medieval City'", she examined some of his concepts. The medieval guild and its extension, the city, were based on "mutual aid." Members of the guild were considered free, mutually supportive, and self-governing. The guilds bought raw materials and sold finished goods without a middleman. The problems of the medieval city developed because mutual aid was not extended to the larger community, a situation which resulted in division of the population into a ruling class and workers or rich and poor with one strong ruler.[23] Stickley, like Kropotkin and Morris, looked favorably upon the concept of the medieval guild as a means of organizing labor for mutual benefit.

In 1909, Stickley was to advocate another kind of cooperation for mutual benefit using the noted capitalist Andrew Carnegie as his example of the enlightened industrialist. Stickley thought that socialism would not work in the United States although it had a commendable purpose in bettering the condition of the workers and the poor. He felt that Carnegie's plan to distribute shares in United States Steel to his workers would provide better work incentives and foster good labor-management relations. He quoted from Carnegie's book *The Problems of Today* (1908):

> We are just at the beginning of profit-sharing, and the reign of workingmen proprietors, which many indications point to as the next step forward in the march of wage-paid labor to the higher stage of profit-sharing, joint partnerships; workers with the hand and workers with the head paid from profits—no dragging of the latter down, but the raising of the former up.

37

Stickley saw as the one flaw of the Carnegie plan the guarantee that the employee would not lose money on his shares of stock, believing instead that the employee must gain or lose on his stock to be a real partner in the company. The idea of profit-sharing as an alternative to socialism appealed to him although he had discontinued his own United Crafts profit-sharing in 1904. He concluded his article on a hopeful note:

> Such a peaceable adjustment would not be to the liking of the ex-treme Socialist or the professional agitator, but would it not be more to the benefit of humanity as a whole than a social upheaval which could end only in confusion and disorder? The laboring man is bound in any case to come to his own. The upward trend of our civilization is irresistible.[24]

In keeping with his idea of the nobility of work, Stickley was a propo-nent of manual training, that is, education in wood and metal shops in public schools. The goal of manual training was not especially the training of children to be good factory workers but rather to provide children with the experience of hand work at the same time they were being exposed to intellectual work. In order to train the child to build, and also to encourage the home craftsman, Stickley published a series of measured drawings of furniture (plate 12) to be copied. That these furniture drawings were very much like his own Craftsman furniture did not seem to bother him. He was apparently more interested in encouraging manual training than in protecting the market for his furniture. In addition to the series on furniture building, Stickley published designs for metal lamps, very like his own Craftsman fixtures, to be built by his readers (plate 13).

The concept of manual training was strongly advocated by Oscar Lovell Triggs (1865–1930), who saw the movement as a means of educating the whole person, be he rich or poor, and counteracting the divisiveness of modern life:

> I can see only one remedy for the class system of modern society — that is, to reconstruct the institutions that embody the social spirit; to create a school which is not so far removed from the workshop as to obliterate real processes and objects — to create a workshop which shall be so fully educative in itself that it will be a virtual school.

12. Chair, *The Craftsman* 5, no. 4 (January 1904): 408.

Triggs proposed the creation of the school in the work place as well as the workshop in the school:

> The failure of the present school is that it exercises the mind, but stops at the point where thought tends to pass out into action.... The

39

failure of the present workshop, in its turn, is that it employs the motor energies, but does not admit of original design. In both cases the education is partial, and so far as I can see, the education of the school is as imperfect as that of the factory.... I do not care whether you introduce manual training into the school, or whether you carry freedom to the factory. The modification of either institution in the direction I have indicated will result in the new workshop which educative industrialism demands.[25]

Certainly craftsmanship and the means of training the craftsman were major parts of the Arts and Crafts Movement as it appeared in *The Craftsman.*

While manual training articles were published only in the early years of *The Craftsman,* gardening articles appear in many issues, the greatest concentration being in 1910–16, possibly because Stickley was then living at Craftsman Farms in Morris Plains, New Jersey, and thus more interested in gardening himself at that point. Although the subjects of manual training and gardening might seem completely unrelated, each had a place in *The Craftsman,* and both subjects were treated on two levels, the theoretical and the practical. Just as readers could learn how to build furniture, they could learn how to grow mushrooms, orchids, or peonies. They could also read articles on landscaping; the relatively small suburban site was emphasized as opposed to the farm or the urban setting.

An article written in 1910 illustrates the scope of the garden according to the Craftsman principles of utility, economy of effort, and beauty. It describes plans for four suburban sites ranging in size from $75' \times 110'$ to $175' \times 225'$ containing houses about 40 feet square. On these sites, a vegetable garden, orchard, lawn and flower borders could be grown without outside help. The list of suggested vegetables is extensive: peas, beets, beans, onions, carrots, spinach, radishes, lima beans, parsley, turnips, tomatoes, lettuce, asparagus, corn, squash, cabbage, muskmelons, and watermelons! In addition to all those vegetables, berries and grapes were suggested. A list of flowers for each of the sites is based on the color of the house and the season in which the garden would be at its prime.[26]

Japanese gardens were the subjects of several *Craftsman* articles, among them a Japanese garden located in Golden Gate Park in San Francisco. The author stressed the contemplative, associative aspects of the oriental garden where one imagines giant mountains in small hills or clouds in banks of

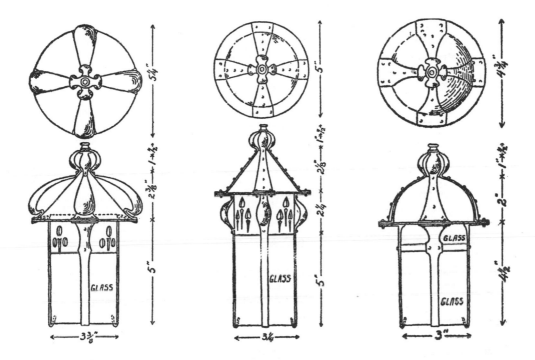

13. Lanterns, *The Craftsman* 4, no. 1 (April 1903).

wisteria. As opposed to the practical gardening articles full of advice, this one focuses on the theoretical framework of the Japanese garden with its illusionistic space concepts and such devices as moving water, bridges, natural rocks, and lanterns to create an atmosphere.[27]

In addition to gardens, many other facets of Japanese life and art were *Craftsman* subjects. Articles on Japanese art were especially prominent in early volumes; Japanese prints, book illustrations, ceramics, bronzes, swords, and boxes were discussed within a historical framework. Readers could even discover the delights of sake and Japanese cooking!

The life style of the preindustrial Japanese craftsman was as much admired as his products. M. L. Wakeman Curtis paid a loving tribute to the Japanese craftsman who lived and worked in beauty:

> Where a nation of people express their highest spiritual attainment
> through an art or craft, the workman will inevitably achieve fitting
> surroundings for his toil, and all unconsciously the laborer himself
> and his workshop will illustrate the beauty he finds in his own soul
> and seeks to express in his work.[28]

Curtis was alarmed at the changes then taking place in Japan as its industries
became westernized and the small home workshop became less common. The
theme of the craftsman in his home workshop reoccurs periodically in *The
Craftsman* as a facet of Stickley's concern for the whole person.

Japan was seen as an inspiration for the American home builder.
Japanese architecture was admired for its simplicity, interrelationship with
nature, and unobtrusive quality. The elimination of extraneous furniture and
ornaments was applauded.[29] In general, Japan and things Japanese appeared in
The Craftsman because the simplicity and harmony of Japanese life were
qualities admired by Stickley.

Stickley had an interest in many ethnic groups. Articles on Chinese,
Hungarian, Czechoslovakian, and Swedish arts and crafts appeared in *The
Craftsman.* He was especially interested in American Indians. In 1904, he took
his wife and two of his daughters on a tour to the western United States,
sending articles back to *The Craftsman* as he traveled. He visited a Yuma
Indian reservation and urged a renewal of traditional Indian life in a conversa-
tion with the superintendent of the reservation:

> In pursuance of this point I expressed my sincere belief in
> the advantages of primitive simplicity over certain features of our too
> artificial life; condemning the policy of depriving a people of the
> handicrafts which they have slowly developed from their necessities,
> and still pursue with the fervor and keen intelligence born of such
> conditions.[30]

The romantic idea of the American Indian as the noble savage in a
simple and primitive society is implicit in *Craftsman* articles on Indian crafts.
Freedom of individual expression in labor, a basic premise of the Arts and
Crafts Movement, was much admired in Indian life.

In vain do our educators anticipate, as a result of the socialistic uplifting of labor, the modern workman's conscious joy in the digging of a ditch. A man can take only so much satisfaction in his labor as shall correspond to the personal intention which it expresses.

The Pima Indian knew that joy, when years before the coming of the white man, he dug his irrigating ditch, and watched the life-giving water flow from level to level as his inventive skill had decreed.

To stand shoulder to shoulder with other hired laborers digging a trench under the direction of a "boss," can give a man no possible cause for satisfaction. This condition is a mental result and can not be induced from without.

Let our students of industrial conditions consider the factors of primitive industry, and reproduce them so far as is possible in modern life. Only by an effectual resistance to the leveling tendencies of industrial organization, as at present practised, only by a return to the freedom of individual expression, can we regain that blessing to the craftsman, the lost joy in labor.[31]

The reestablishment of "the lost joy in labor" as well as the craft products of that labor was a goal of the Arts and Crafts Movement and a theme which appears in many contexts in *The Craftsman*. Stickley admired the early Indian life style as much as their crafts.

Stickley liked the mission architecture of California with its balconies and courtyards which he saw as well suited to the climate of the state. In Riverside, California, he and his family stayed at the mission style Glenwood Hotel which he described, comparing it to Moorish architecture in Spain and street facades in Italy. As might be expected, it was the simplicity of the hotel's structure which appealed to him.[32] The Glenwood Hotel may have been suggested to Stickley by George Wharton James (1858–1923), associate editor of *The Craftsman* 1904–1905. An earlier *Craftsman* article by James on Spanish missions as a design source for modern California buildings had been illustrated with photographs of the hotel as well as other mission revival buildings.[33]

The elements which unite such diverse Craftsman themes as socialism, manual training, gardening, Japan, American Indians, and California missions have to do with Stickley's belief in mutual cooperation as a way of life and simplicity as a goal of that life style. He never gave up those beliefs. They were implicit throughout the pages of *The Craftsman* and in Stickley's own designs. It is the diversity of approaches to the Craftsman philosophy which makes his magazine so readable even now, and it is the same diversity of interests which made Gustav Stickley such an interesting man.

4

THE CRAFTSMAN EMPIRE EXPANDS

HE YEARS 1902–1905 were of seminal importance to Gustav Stickley since it was during those years that he became interested in architecture, made contact with Harvey Ellis, and evolved his mature Craftsman furniture.

It is hardly surprising that Stickley as a furniture designer desired an ideal interior environment for his furniture. He rejected the typical house of the early twentieth century as too heavily decorated for his straight-lined, unornamented Craftsman pieces. In his search for the ideal totally designed environment, he had such inspirational models as William Morris' Red House at Bexley Heath, which was designed by Phillip Webb, and houses designed by Baillie Scott and Voysey.

Stickley, untrained in architecture, began with furniture design and expanded his design horizons to include houses while his English counterparts, all trained as architects, had become involved in furniture design because they were unable to find proper furniture for the houses they designed or inhabited. Because of his furniture design background, Stickley was always more interested in interiors than in exterior design, and it is in Craftsman interiors that he did his best architectural work. Since Stickley's interests and enthusiasms were reflected in *The Craftsman,* his magazine began to feature occasional house designs which became a monthly feature in 1904.

The opportunity for Stickley to experiment with the ideal interior came about as the result of an extensive fire which broke out in his own home on Christmas Eve 1902. After a complete remodeling, his house was so changed and such a perfect background for his own furniture that it might be called the first Craftsman house, at least as far as the interior is concerned. Built in 1900 on Columbus Avenue in Syracuse[1] (plate 14) his house has such typical neo-colonial details as corner pilasters and a swan's neck pediment over a second floor triple window. There is no indication that Stickley had any part in the design of the unremarkable exterior. The entry porch has been changed since Stickley's remodeling, and it is now impossible to know its

14, 15. Gustav Stickley house, Syracuse, New York, exterior, 1900, and door, c. 1902. Photographs by Mary Ann Smith.

original design. Only the remodeled bay window and front door (plate 15) are unusual for their period. Both are typical of late nineteenth-century English Arts and Crafts houses. Stickley could have easily seen similar details in Baillie Scott and Voysey Houses in periodicals or during his 1898 trip to England.[2]

    The broad front door of the house is made of oak originally finished like his furniture; the panes of amber hammered glass are repeated in many of the house's interior doors. The door's hardware, repeated in later Craftsman houses, is heavy, wrought metal; a large ring substitutes for a doorknob. The stridently rectilinear door framing is softened somewhat by the curving corbels, a detail used by Stickley on a smaller scale as arm supports for some of his Craftsman chairs. This detail may have been inspired by an illustration of a staircase designed by Baillie Scott which appeared in *International Studio* in 1898.[3] However, Baillie Scott had used it as a supporting element for ceiling beams. Stickley's nonfunctional use of this detail is unusual since he believed strongly that all design details should be structural and not simply ornamental. Its use here is another indication that this house represents a transitional stage in his design concepts.

At the turn of the century, there was little to inspire Stickley in American architectural periodicals. Such eastern periodicals as *American Architect and Building News* and *Architectural Record* were not concerned with the design of middle class houses; instead, they featured such classically inspired nondomestic buildings as McKim, Mead and White's Law Library of Columbia University and Carrère and Hastings' New York Public Library. The houses illustrated were large and expensive, often of half-timbered Tudor style. The *Architectural Review* of Boston, another rather conservative periodical, did publish an article by Robert C. Spencer on Frank Lloyd Wright[4] which Stickley could have seen. However, in view of Stickley's later lack of interest in Wright's work, we can assume that he would not have been impressed by the article if he had seen it. Stickley may have been familiar with *Inland Architect and News Record*, published in Chicago, which illustrated houses by Myron Hunt and others, but its articles seem to have had no direct influence on him, at least at this time.

Of all American periodicals *The House Beautiful,* published in Chicago, had the greatest impact on Stickley. The magazine had featured his furniture editorially as well as in the Tobey advertisements,[5] and thus he surely would have been aware of its articles on houses. *The House Beautiful* was not simply an architectural journal; from the start, it had carried articles on the Arts and Crafts Movement in England and the United States. It also occasionally featured the relatively small house type later to be published in the *Craftsman* with the same kind of detailed descriptions and illustrations of interiors. For example, "A Small House" by Spencer Roberts (February 1898), had a general similarity to Stickley's house with beamed ceilings, small-paned windows, rough brick fireplace, built-in cabinets, and expansive staircase. Other *House*

Beautiful interiors of the 1890s had a general similarity to Stickley's house although there seems to have been no one house which was the prototype for his house or its details.

It was the details of English Arts and Crafts houses and those in *The House Beautiful* which Stickley emulated. The floor plans of his house (plate 16) owe nothing to English precedents and very little to earlier American houses. Within the constraints of a narrow site, the house's ground floor plan has a considerable openness while retaining a sense of privacy for family activities. To reach the living room, a visitor must make two left turns, a planning device Frank Lloyd Wright had used for the same purpose in several of his Prairie houses such as the Harley Bradley house in Kankakee, Illinois (1900), and the Ward Willits house in Highland Park, Illinois (1902). A visitor can barely see the dining room and the library behind it from the entry because a folding screen obscures the view, yet anyone seated within the living room bay window area can see all the way through the house to the library, a distance of some sixty-six feet.

Essentially the stair hall, dominated by a large staircase, (plate 17) acts as a cross axis joining the two parallel axes from the front to the back of the house. The large hall also serves as an overflow space for the living room since there is a large opening between the two areas. The idea of the large hall used as a living space rather than for circulation only comes from English Queen Anne houses via American houses of the Shingle style. From the late 1870s until the period of Stickley's house, the hall, often the largest room in the house complete with fireplace and an ample staircase, served as a family living space while the parlor or drawing room was reserved for formal occasions.[6] Although Stickley's hall was larger than his living room, it was not used as a living room substitute but rather as an extension of the main living area.

Stickley's Craftsman houses, beginning with this one, did not have formal parlors or drawing rooms. He believed that the house should be used by all family members without reserving formal rooms for the entertainment of guests. Indeed, the concept of the living room as substitute for the formal parlor was popularized by him. In the early twentieth century a den was a hideaway for the man of the house, and the "family room" of the second half of the century was unknown. While it is true that the open area beside the staircase on the second floor was used as a playroom by his children, he expected those children to also use the living room along with the adults.

The interior of Stickley's house resembles his furniture so strongly that

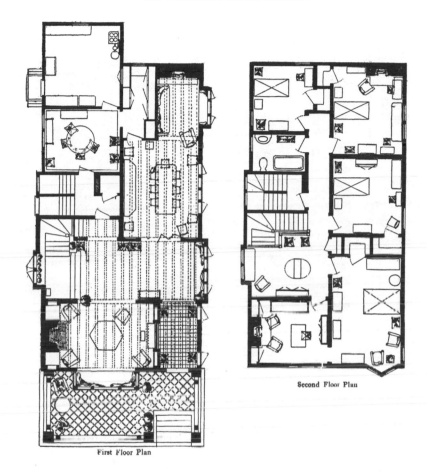

First Floor Plan

Second Floor Plan

16. Gustav Stickley house, Syracuse, New York, c. 1902, floor plans. *The Craftsman* 3, no. 3 (February 1903). 162–63.

its design can be attributed to him with certainty. The ground floor is a unified open space with rooms divided only slightly by structural supports. Two elements reinforce the openness of the plan. First, a horizontal band at the level of the tops of doors and windows connects all the walls of the ground

17. Gustav Stickley house, Syracuse, New York, c. 1902, hall. *The Craftsman* 3, no. 3 (February 1903): 164.

floor. Below the band walls are paneled with vertical boards; above it, they are plastered. Second, the rectangular ceiling beams, parallel to the sides of the house, are used from the front to the rear, emphasizing the perspective view from living room to hall to dining room to library and the openness of the continuous spaces (plates 18 and 19). In contrast to the usual house of the early 1900s, there are no curved or carved moldings. There is nothing extraneous; instead, there are structural supports and beams frankly exposed.

18. Gustav Stickley house, Syracuse, New
York, c. 1902, living room. *The Craftsman* 3,
no. 3 (February 1903): 161.

19. Gustav Stickley house, Syracuse, New York, c.
1902, dining room and library. Photograph by
Mary Ann Smith.

The only differentiation of rooms is the structural cross beams which separate spaces visually. Samuel Howe, writing about this house in a February 1903 *Craftsman* article, commented on the simple structural character of the house:

> The square impost which marks the entrance to dining room and library, denotes a very much plainer, franker use of structural features than is usual. It looks really able to support the house. The scale is big —it thrills. It has neither base nor cap, even that would be a mistake. The composition is stronger as it is.... Not alone is this house remarkable because of its conspicuous absence of carving, molding, and inlay by way of ornament, but because of the singularly frank manner in which they have been omitted. No false construction is allowed to take the place of these popular idols by presenting rudely wrought, primitive forms as an architectural expedient.[7]

Stickley's living room was a perfect place to try out his ideas of structural simplicity. The red brick fireplace has a recessed mantle shelf with a heavy stone lintel. The fireplace opening is surmounted by a small metal hood, a device which is both decorative and practical. Stickley, who liked built-ins to simplify housekeeping and free rooms of excess furniture, used glass-doored cabinets on either side of the fireplace and a long bay window seat in his living room. The light fixtures and much of the furniture used in this house were designed especially for it by Stickley and produced in his workshops. Perhaps he tried out new furniture here before producing it for public sale.

The second story of the house is notable for several of its details. The sitting room adjoining the master bedroom in the front of the house has a fireplace (plate 20) faced with Grueby tiles and bounded with brass bands as does the fireplace in one of the other bedrooms. These plain fireplaces are reminiscent of Voysey and Baillie Scott. The walls of the second-story hall (plate 21) are divided into bays by naturally finished planks with curved corbels like those used for the house's front door. Bedroom walls have similarly divided surfaces but no corbels. Unlike the ground floor woodwork, the bedroom woodwork was apparently always painted.

When Stickley's family moved away from this house to Morris Plains, New Jersey, in 1911, it was sold with several unique stipulations; the furniture

20. Gustav Stickley house, Syracuse, New York, c. 1902, fireplace. Photograph by Mary Ann Smith.

21. Gustav Stickley house, Syracuse, New York, c. 1902, second floor hall. *The Craftsman* 3, no. 3 (February 1903): 165.

22. One-room suburban house, 1902, exterior. *The Craftsman* 2, no. 5 (August 1902): 242.

was sold with the house and was to remain in it. Furthermore, Stickley retained an option to repurchase the house and its contents. The house and its furniture were bought by Stickley's daughter Barbara and her husband, Ben Wiles, in 1919, and Gustav Stickley spent the last years of his life in it.[8]

When Stickley's house was published in *The Craftsman* in February 1903, the only exterior illustration was a sketch of the front door, an indication that Stickley did not consider the exterior worthy of notice. He had earlier published the first house to appear in *The Craftsman* in August 1902. Called a "one-room suburban house" (plate 22) and probably designed by Stickley, this house is amateurish at best. The idea of open living space, the "one-room" living-dining room of the title, to visually enlarge the square footage of the

"The Craftsman House"   Designed by E. G. W. Dietrich

23. Craftsman house, E. G. W. Dietrich and Gustav Stickley, 1903, exterior. *The Craftsman* 4, no. 2 (May 1903): following 84.

small house was to be often repeated in later Craftsman houses. Irene Sargent wrote a brief description of color schemes for the house,[9] a feature of most later Craftsman house articles in which interior design was of great importance.

  After publishing the rather unsuccessful "one-room" house and successfully remodeling his own house, Stickley probably realized that he needed the services of a trained architect as a collaborator to actualize the Craftsman house as an entity with the exterior as well designed as the interior. He hired architect Ernest G. W. Dietrich (1857–1924), and together they designed the first house to be labeled Craftsman (plate 23). It appeared in *The Craftsman* in May 1903, just three months after Stickley's own house. The overall design and

24. Craftsman house, E. G. W. Dietrich and Gustav Stickley, 1903, library. *The Craftsman* 4, no. 2 (May 1903): following 87.

the exterior rendering were surely Dietrich's contribution since the general form of the house with a gambrel roof enclosing the second story and attic was similar to other Dietrich houses. Had the exterior been shingled rather than built of fieldstone, it would have fit nicely into the colonializing phase of the shingle style. Moreover, this first Craftsman house had the typical shingle style living hall instead of a living room.

Stickley probably designed the interior based in part on experience in his house remodeling; the illustrations of the interior, obviously not by the delineator of the exterior, are done in the same style as the "one-room suburban house." The library (plate 24) features a Stickley armchair and round table, high-backed inglenook seats like those in his library, and built-in cabinets with strap hinges. The slightly curved corbels and the shuttered windows with small stained-glass inserts are reminiscent of Baillie Scott as is the fireplace design with tiles on either side of the hood.[10]

The very specific description of interiors makes them easy to visualize. On the ground floor woodwork was to be chestnut treated with ammonia and then lacquered; ceilings and the wall area above the horizontal moldings were to have a white sand finish, while the lower part of the walls would be covered with "hempen textile" of a variegated greenish yellow color. Copper-hooded fireplaces of Harvard brick set in black mortar were recommended for the ground floor, and Grueby tile was suggested for bedroom fireplaces as in Stickley's house. The description ended with an editor's note offering help to any subscriber who wanted details on the "building, finishing or decorating of 'The Craftsman House'".[11] The two elements of this first Craftsman house article which carry through to later house articles are the detailed interior description, much more complete than exterior description, and the offer to provide information to subscribers. Stickley obviously wanted his readers to have houses with a Craftsman ambience and was willing to spend time addressing the questions they might have to help achieve the proper home atmosphere. Readers responded to his offer and occasionally their letters and his answers were printed in *The Craftsman*.

For a brief but very productive seven-month period from June 1903 to January 1904, Stickley was fortunate to have in his employ an architect named Harvey Ellis (1852–1904). Called a shadowy figure by all who have written about him,[12] Ellis was an alcoholic, erratic, and probably unstable, but most importantly a genius in design. Born in Rochester, New York, in 1852, Ellis won an appointment to West Point in 1870 but stayed there only a year. He then spent several years in Europe, returning to the United States to join the architectural office of Henry Hobson Richardon in 1877–78, while Richardson was working on the City Hall and New York State Capitol in Albany. In 1879, Ellis returned to Rochester to work with his architect brother, Charles.

During the late 1880s and early 1890s, Harvey Ellis worked as a delineator and designer, drifting from one architectural office to another. In Minnesota, he worked for J. Walter Stevens and Leroy Buffington in the late 1880s. While employed by Buffington in 1887, he contributed substantially to the design of a twenty-nine story skyscraper, never built, which led Buffington to claim invention of the first steel framed tall building. From 1888 to 1893, he worked for Edmund J. Eckel and George R. Mann in Missouri.[13]

Since Ellis' designs were usually attributed to his employers, it is difficult to know just what he did design. He was even called a "paper architect" whose work was never built.[14] However, it seems likely that a number of building designs signed by his employers were Ellis'. His fine architectural renderings in pen and ink or watercolor were much admired by his contemporaries. William Grant Elmslie, an architectural protégé of Louis Sullivan, wrote of Ellis:

> No American artist had a more perfect technical language for architectural rendering.... His name was well known to everyone who read an architectural magazine from 1880 to well past 1900.[15]

Ellis' friend Claude Bragdon, who credited Ellis along with Louis Sullivan as his main sources of inspiration, wrote:

> The strong-nerved young draughtsmen of the Middle West used to nick the edges of their T-squares in the effort to reproduce Harvey's crinkled pen-line — the product, did they but know it, of nerves unstrung.[16]

Harvey Ellis had become largely disillusioned with architecture by 1895 when he rejoined his brother, Charles in Rochester, preferring to paint pictures inspired by the Japanese prints he collected. His watercolors followed the "charcoal school" of the Japanese in that they had bold ink outlines in which watercolor pigments were applied over "notan" areas in values from light to dark charcoal.[17] This technique which gave his watercolors depth while preserving two-dimensional flatness of surface was to be used effectively when he joined Stickley's staff.

Ellis brought a solid architectural background and special skills in rendering to his new position at the Crouse Stables in 1903. When their association began Stickley had probably just completed the interior of his own house, and he had recently published the first Craftsman house designed with Dietrich's help. At this point he probably had a fairly clear idea of what Craftsman houses should be, and he clearly had an interest in developing houses for his magazine. Although Craftsman houses were to appear in all sizes from tiny cottages to large mansions and their designs were to be influenced by

English Arts and Crafts houses, Tudor, Prairie School, and even oriental architecture, there was always the Stickley touch. The Craftsman house which was to evolve with Ellis' help and to continue after his departure was thus already in the formative stage when he arrived upon the scene. Ellis' real contribution, aside from his designs for Stickley, was to be the inspiration he provided at a critical point in Stickley's development. It is not clear whether Ellis was hired to design Craftsman houses or furniture although it seems likely that he was employed primarily as an architect. As his job evolved, he designed houses, furniture, wall decorations, and illustrations for *The Craftsman.*

The first Harvey Ellis Craftsman house (plate 25) appeared in July 1903. Its asymmetry, steeply pitched roof, and rough cast exterior immediately bring to mind the English Arts and Crafts houses of Baillie Scott and Voysey, and yet it is no mere copy of any of their designs. Since Ellis had not been to Europe since the late 1870s, it seems clear that this remarkably English-looking house must have been inspired by those same periodicals such as *Studio* and *The House Beautiful* which had influenced Stickley. In common with other architects, Ellis clipped articles on American, English, and French buildings from magazines. He probably shared Stickley's Arts and Crafts philosophy since he owned a copy of John Ruskin's *Seven Lamps of Architecture*[18] and his favorite author was William Morris.[19] Ellis' rendering technique, very similar to Baillie Scott's makes the house seem even more English.

This was a house to be built for $4,000 on a restricted site of 50 feet frontage. The text of his article delineates the steps necessary in planning the house and describes the interior. The most interesting room of the house is the great room or hall (plate 26) with a fireplace flanked by a built-in seat. The heavy woodwork, small-paned casement window, and fireplace resemble details of the slightly earlier Dietrich-Stickley house (plate 24), but there is an elegance and an emptiness here missing in the earlier house. The point of view of Ellis' rendering provided him with the opportunity to design an arras tapestry for one wall. The hanging light fixtures and table are Stickley's designs.

The dining room (plate 27) is also furnished with Stickley's furniture. Ellis, who was preoccupied with color relationships, painted a bright word picture of this room:

> Here, the walls are a strong golden yellow, the ceiling the gray of the plaster, and the woodwork a rich olive green; the visible wall in the alcove for the sideboard is a dark, dull Indian red, and the floor a

25. Craftsman house, Harvey Ellis, 1903, exterior. *The Craftsman* 4, no. 4 (July 1903): following 268.

26. Craftsman house, Harvey Ellis, 1903, great room. *The Craftsman* 4, no. 4 (July 1903): following 276.

golden yellow, with a large moss-green rug in the center. Extending about the room is a small pseudo-frieze, which has for its color a bright Venetian red. The windows are hung with a fabric akin to India silk, whose color is, largely, a creamy white, old rose and gold. The leaded window over the sideboard is framed with broad bands of blackened copper; while the martins in the designs are of a dark gray

27. Craftsman house, Harvey Ellis, 1903, dining room. *The Craftsman* 4, no. 4 (July 1903): facing 277.

blue, with circles or halos about their heads of a bright yellow, and all against a background of cloudy milk-colored opaque glass, which has faint streaks of dull turquoise blue running through it.[20]

The vivid description of the subtly colored leaded glass window above the dining room sideboard indicates that it may have actually existed.[21] Although Ellis' Craftsman houses sometimes featured stained-glass windows, few were incorporated into the Craftsman houses which were built; owners seem to have preferred small-paned casement windows similar to those in Stickley's Syracuse house. The clear windows used in Craftsman houses are a marked contrast to the great variety of stained-glass designs used by Frank Lloyd Wright and his contemporaries in the Midwest.

Ellis considered color schemes for the whole of his first Craftsman house. The hallway was to be a cheerful golden color with a dull violet pot or wallhanging at the end. Asymmetrically hung Japanese prints were suggested for the walls. Blues and greens were thought correct for the kitchen while the bathroom was to be red or yellow. Bedroom walls were to be painted in cool colors on the southwestern side of the house and in warm shades on the northwest; small objects in complementary colors were to be used for contrast. Ellis, whose main interest in the years before he joined the *Craftsman* staff had been his painting, clearly brought his painterly imagination to bear when he wrote about this house.

During his employment in Syracuse, almost every issue of *The Craftsman* contained an Ellis building. They ranged from a chapel to an Adirondack lodge; each appeared with a careful interior description and Ellis' masterly illustrations. His design for August 1903, an urban house (plate 28), unusual in *The Craftsman* which usually featured country and suburban houses, was one of Ellis' best contributions to the magazine. This was no small country cottage but rather a large, six-bedroom city house planned to use every foot of its restricted site (plate 29). A wall at the front edge of the site protects the privacy of an entrance terrace, and the raised front porch is screened from public view. The "auto way," a place to park the family car, must have been unusual in 1903, when relatively few people owned cars. The living room, compartmented to included a music room and a secluded inglenook, has large windows facing the walled front terrace and the rear porch and formal garden. The second-story bedrooms face the rear garden, a design device

28. Urban house, Harvey Ellis, 1903, exterior. *The Craftsman* 4, no. 5 (August 1903): following 312.

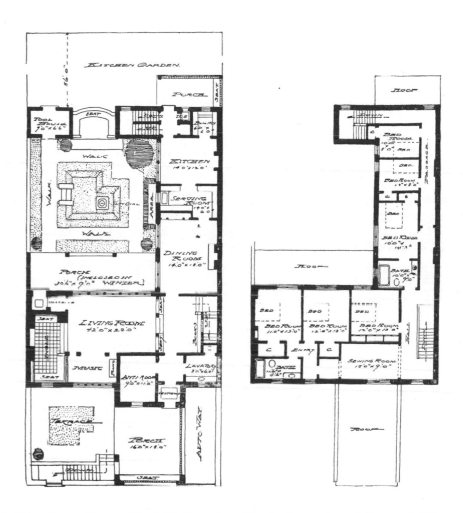

29. Urban house, Harvey Ellis, 1903, floor plans. *The Craftsman 4,* no. 5 (August 1903): following 313.

H. H. Richardson had used in his Glessner house (1885–87) on an urban Chicago site.

The living room (plate 30) is one of Ellis' finest designs. Although the rectilinear posts, beams, and built-in seats are pure Stickley, the ornamentation of wall surfaces with stylized floral designs is Ellis' own, obviously inspired by the Art Nouveau motifs of Charles Rennie Mackintosh and the Glasgow school. These graceful linear designs seem to fill the room, otherwise unfurnished. However, the music room, just visible on the left, contains an Ellis-designed music cabinet.

In November 1903, *The Craftsman* announced the formation of a Home Builders' Club for its readers. Any subscriber was eligible to order a free set of house plans for any one of a series of houses to be published in *The Craftsman* each month during 1904. The houses were expected to cost from $2,000 to $5,000. Thus began Stickley's attempt to spread his Craftsman message in a tangible way to his friends, the readers. The Craftsman houses for which free plans were available were to number more than two hundred before the magazine ceased publication in 1916. In some issues there were several plans. Harvey Ellis may have suggested the Home Builders' Club to Stickley; it was an idea which appealed to Stickley's apostolic personality.

The first of the Home Builders' Club houses (plate 31) which was published in January 1904, seems to have been designed by Harvey Ellis although it was not signed with his initials in a circle like his other house designs. The watercolor wash rendering technique used for the exterior illustration resembles Ellis's earlier work for *The Craftsman*. This was one of the few Craftsman houses in the California mission style and a departure from the earlier Ellis houses in *The Craftsman*. However, 1904 was the year of Stickley's trip to the American west, and he sent back a series of articles to *The Craftsman* about such western topics as Spanish missions, Indians, and California climate. Ellis shared Stickley's interest in mission architecture and perhaps was one of the people who inspired this new enthusiasm of Stickley's. Ellis had visited the southwestern states in the early 1890s[22] and even written a *Craftsman* article on Spanish missions in December 1903, the month before the first Home Builders' house was published. Ellis saw in the Spanish missions a "simple, straightforward solution of an architectural problem," and curiously, the Spanish mission design approach seemed to remind him of Louis Sullivan and other Chicago architects.[23]

30. Urban house, Harvey Ellis, 1903, living room. *The Craftsman* 4, no. 5 (August 1903): following 317.

The Craftsman house exterior with its arched openings, red tile roof, and rough cement walls reflects mission motifs, yet the conventional floor plan of center entrance hall flanked by living room and dining room is not as interesting as that of Ellis's earlier "urban house." When the house was republished in Stickley's *Craftsman Homes* (1910), it had a new accompanying text

31. Craftsman house, number one, series of 1904, Harvey Ellis, exterior. *The Craftsman* 5, no. 4 (January 1904): following 397.

which suggested that other materials might be more appropriately used in different parts of the country. It seems that the house was thought of as being mission style in only the vaguest of terms.

Harvey Ellis also contributed illustrations to *The Craftsman*. Some of his most charming designs illustrate "Puss in Boots, An Old Myth in New

32, 33. "Puss in Boots, An Old Myth in New Dress," 1903, Harvey Ellis, marriage of the king's daughter and wall of nursery. *The Craftsman* 4, no. 5 (August 1903): 379, 380.

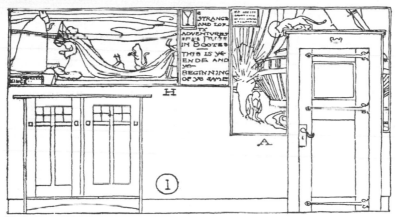

Dress,"[24] which he possibly wrote although the article appeared anonymously. The illustrations, to be used as wall hanging designs for a small child's nursery, depict various stages in Puss' career. The marriage scene showing the king's daughter with Puss in attendance (plate 32), the last of the cycle, has an overlay of sinuous lines and an Art Nouveau quality similar to the floral details used in Ellis' "urban house" living room. The illustration of the whole wall on which the marriage scene would be placed (plate 33) introduces a bookcase probably designed by Ellis to the *Craftsman* public.

In addition to his architectural, illustrative, and written work for *The Craftsman,* Ellis designed furniture for Stickley. Before the advent of Ellis, many of Stickley's designs had been rather heavy; Harvey Ellis' designs were lighter in appearance and more delicately detailed. A comparison of the early Eastwood chair (plate 9) with an armchair Ellis designed for Stickley (plate 34) shows just how different they are. The Stickley armchair seems massive and "primitive," which is just the effect Stickley desired, while the Ellis armchair with its slender slats, curved apron, and stylized flower inlay is more closely related to the furniture of Voysey, Baillie Scott, and Mackintosh. Although Stickley was generally opposed to the use of applied ornament on furniture, he must have approved Ellis' inlay designs which emphasized the structure of the designs. Comparing the ornament on Ellis' furniture to the fluting of columns of a Greek temple, an anonymous *Craftsman* writer, possibly Stickley or Ellis, stated:

> These pieces in every case, boldly assert the purpose for which they are designed. The chair does not reach out after the attributes of the table; nor yet does the round table purloin the characteristics of the square object of its own kind. Each specimen preserves a structural distinction as marked as that which separates, one from the other, the species and varieties of the animal and the vegetable kingdoms. The principles upon which they are based follow Nature, and must therefore be sound and true.... It [decoration] is used, as was decoration with the Greeks, to relieve and make interesting what otherwise would have been a too large area of plain, flat surface. It in every case, emphasizes the structural lines; accenting in most instances the vertical elements, and so giving a certain slenderness of effect to a whole which were otherwise too solid and heavy.[25]

Harvey Ellis died on January 4, 1905, at the age of fifty-two. He had been employed by Stickley for only seven months. However, in that brief period of time and despite his problems with alcohol, he found time to design Craftsman houses, write and illustrate *Craftsman* articles, and design some handsome furniture. Probably none of his Craftsman houses were ever built; his inlaid furniture seems to have been produced in only limited quantities. He was missed but his influence survived him, especially in the Craftsman shops in Eastwood where, for a time, some Craftsman designs reflected the lighter weight and more slender proportions he had introduced.

34. Inlaid armchair, Harvey Ellis for Gustav Stickley, c. 1903–1904. Photograph courtesy of Jordan Volpe Gallery, New York, New York.

A comparison of pre-Ellis Craftsman furniture with pieces designed or influenced by him and those designed after his death shows the changes very well. A side chair with a three-slat back c. 1901 (plate 35) has slightly curved inserts on either side of the back; the curves are repeated in the front and rear stretchers and the top rail of the back. An Ellis-inspired side chair of c. 1903 (plate 36), which is a modification of the inlaid armchair (plate 34) with the upper back rail and inlay omitted, retains the three-slat back of the earlier

71

Craftsman chair (plate 35) but has a taller back and each element is more slender. The slenderness of structural elements is evident also in the stretchers and legs of the Ellis-inspired designs. Stickley did not abandon the sturdy proportions of his furniture after his contact with Ellis as is shown by a four-slat side chair of c. 1905 (plate 37). Here we can see the evolution from the rather massive early chair through the slender Ellis-influenced chair to a kind of happy medium of proportions; the c. 1905 chair is neither as heavy as the very early one nor as light as the Ellis chair. Stickley introduced a line of "spindle" furniture in 1905, phasing it out c. 1910. Although he called the slats "spindles," they were square rather than round.[26] While the spindle-back side chair, c. 1910 (plate 38), is not as delicate as the one inspired by Ellis (plate 36), it is much lighter than the pre-Ellis side chair (plate 35); the back of this late spindle-back chair is somewhat lower than earlier spindle designs, and the stretcher design resembles that of some early Craftsman chairs.

A similar comparison can be made using single-door Craftsman bookcases as examples. A bookcase of c. 1901 (plate 39) has boldly articulated tenon and pin joints and a slatted gallery; the muntins separating the pieces of glass are quite wide. In contrast, a c. 1905 bookcase (plate 40) has much less prominent mortise and tenon joints, thinner muntins, and gentle curves at the sides of the top. An Ellis-inspired bookcase, also c. 1905 (plate 41), has the same delicacy of proportion of his chair designs and a similarly curved apron at its base. Unlike the two bookcases above, the height of the Ellis-inspired design is emphasized by vertical muntins and pseudo columns at either side of the door. The thin overhanging top is reminiscent of Voysey. A double-door version of this bookcase shown in Ellis' "Puss and Boots" *Craftsman* article (plate 33) was also produced at this time. Even while Stickley was manufacturing bookcases, chairs, and other pieces, influenced by Ellis, he was also making his more typically heavy furniture as is evident from the two bookcases manufactured at the same time. There were many pieces of furniture in the Craftsman line so that customers could have a wide choice.

Harvey Ellis designed furniture and houses for Stickley which were radically different from earlier Craftsman designs. He introduced Stickley to new design possibilities and perhaps provided the impetus for Craftsman houses as a regular feature of his magazine. Stickley, who had established the basic characteristics of the Craftsman interior before Ellis' seven months on

35, 36. Side chairs, Gustav Stickley, c. 1901 (left), and c. 1903 (right). Photographs by Rick Echelmeyer, courtesy of The Artsman, Bryn Mawr, Pennsylvania.

37, 38. Side chairs, Gustav Stickley, c. 1905 (left), and c. 1910 (right). Photographs by Rick Echelmeyer, courtesy of The Artsman, Bryn Mawr, Pennsylvania.

39, 40, 41. Single-door bookcases, Gustav Stickley, c. 1901 (left), c. 1905 (center), and c. 1905 (right). Plates 39 and 40 photographs by Rick Echelmeyer, courtesy of The Artsman, Bryn Mawr, Pennsylvania; plate 41 photograph by E. P. A., 342 Madison Avenue, New York

the scene, was to benefit from the Ellis touch as he further developed the Craftsman house — the ideal middle class environment for the simple, high-minded life style he promoted in *The Craftsman*.

5

THE CRAFTSMAN HOME BUILDERS' CLUB

HE CRAFTSMAN HOME BUILDERS' CLUB, begun after Ellis' death in 1904, became an increasingly imporant feature of *The Craftsman*. In each issue devoted readers could find at least one house with plans to be ordered from the magazine. It is impossible to know how many subscribers ordered plans or used published plans since no list of loyal adherents to the Craftsman style exists. In 1915, Stickley claimed that more than $20 million dollars had been spent in that year alone to build Craftsman houses in all parts of the United States and as far afield as Alaska and the Fiji Islands.[1] From this we must conclude that Craftsman houses were popular and that many people ordered plans, especially if we remember that the average Craftsman house cost well under $10,000, and in some cases the houses cost less than $5,000.

The free Craftsman plans contained enough details to make construction of the houses possible by local contractors. Typically the plans included exterior elevations (plate 42), dimensioned floor plans (plate 43), and interior details or sections (plate 44). The local carpenter could follow the plans or adapt them according to the client's wishes. Craftsman light fixtures and hardware could be ordered for the house, and woodwork could be finished according to directions printed in *The Craftsman* for finishing homemade furniture. Since Craftsman woodwork was essentially beautifully finished flat boards, it would be simple to make anywhere, its final appearance dependent on the variety of wood used and its finish. The quality of the completed house would depend on the skills of the local builders and the materials used.

Stickley was interested in the small cottage or bungalow which most Americans could afford. There was some English Arts and Crafts influence on the picturesque early Craftsman houses with their steeply pitched roof lines and small-paned, grouped windows, yet the wood-shingled exteriors and the porches which were an important feature of the cottages were American. A 1906 Craftsman cottage (plate 45) has all these features. The house is close to the ground, its horizontality emphasized by the flat dormer and the porch

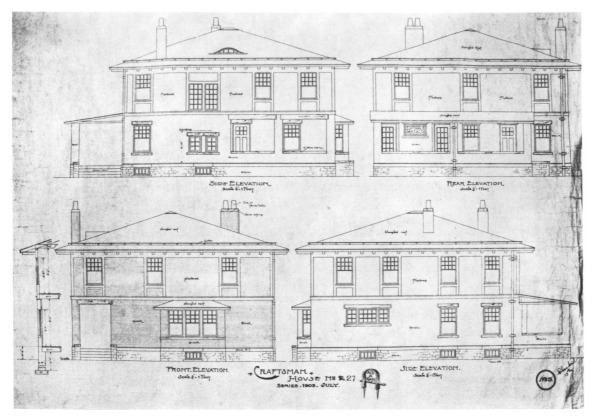

42. Craftsman house, number twenty-seven, series of 1905, July, elevations. Avery Architectural and Fine Arts Library, Columbia University.

which stretches across the facade. The floor plan (plate 46) is quite open with only a partial partition between living room and dining room; thus even in this small house the living-dining space is thirty-nine feet in length. Most Craftsman houses have built-in seating of some sort; here the only furnishing of the small vestibule is a short, built-in seat. Another built-in seat is planned for the bay window opposite the fireplace. The living room, furnished with a Craftsman

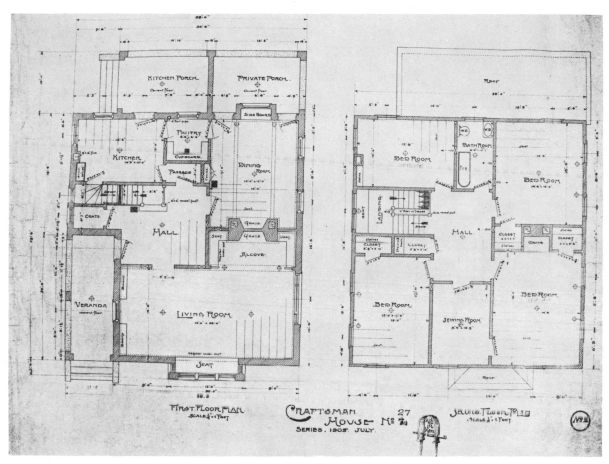

43. Craftsman house, number twenty-seven, series of 1905, July, floor plans. Avery Architectural and Fine Arts Library, Columbia University.

armchair, table, and settle, is to have pine woodwork stained moss green and a darker green floor (plate 47); the reader is cautioned that a Craftsman house should not have solid colored woodwork but rather stain finishes so that

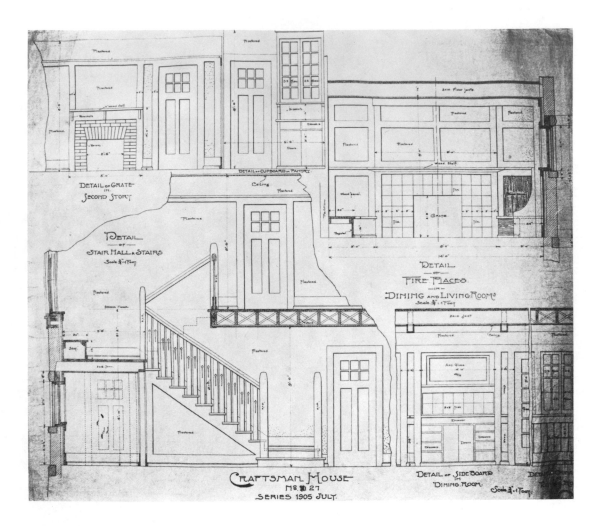

44. Craftsman house, number twenty-seven, series of 1905, July, interior details. Avery Architectural and Fine Arts Library, Columbia University.

45, 46. Craftsman house, number two, series of 1906, exterior and floor plans. *The Craftsman* 9, no. 5 (February 1906): 715, 717.

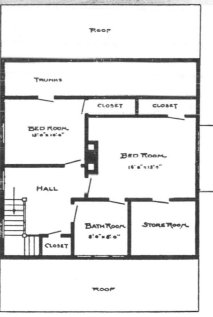

SECOND FLOOR

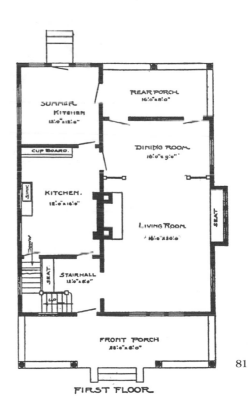

FIRST FLOOR

81

47. Craftsman house, number two, series of 1906, living room. *The Craftsman* 9, no. 5 (February 1906): following 714.

woodgrain shows. The suggested wall color is yellow verging on brown or Byzantine gold with a stenciled frieze of green and peach.[2] The green to yellow color scheme is typical of Craftsman houses where the tonality of nature was preferred.

Whether or not small Craftsman houses could be called bungalows depends on what one means by the word "bungalow." Certainly bungalows were very popular in the United States while the Craftsman house was being popularized and some small Craftsman houses were called bungalows in the magazine. "Bungalow" is derived from "bangala" and means "of or belonging to Bengali." In the nineteenth century and perhaps earlier, the word had been used to refer to a gabled native hut. The native Indian bungalow was gradually modified for use by Europeans in India. Verandas or porches were common. The Indian bungalow, generally one story high on a very low foundation, had a large living-dining room and small bedrooms. During the nineteenth century, the Anglo-Indian bungalow was thought of as a temporary or vacation house for the hot season.[3] This bungalow type had all the basic elements which eventually became part of the American bungalow in the early twentieth century. Although the means of transmitting the Indian bungalow house type are unclear, many bungalows were being constructed in California by the early 1900s, probably because the open plan, porches, and closeness to the ground suited the California climate so well.[4] Bungalows were also considered to be inexpensive to construct, an added advantage of the house type.

Gustav Stickley took his family on a trip to California in 1904[5] at just the time the bungalow was achieving popularity there. It seems likely that he met Charles Sumner Greene (1868–1957) and Henry Mather Greene (1870–1954) during this trip or at least saw their Bandini house (1903) in Pasadena and their Hollister house (1904) in Hollywood. The evidence of a connection is a Craftsman house published in July 1904 (plate 48). Although the exterior with its two prominent stone chimneys and curving entrance porch has little resemblance to any Greene and Greene houses, the courtyard plan (plate 49) is almost a copy of the Hollister plan reversed. The Craftsman house even has a pool in the same location as that of the Hollister house. From the Bandini house Stickley could have derived the idea of the porch around three sides of the courtyard. In the text describing the house the exterior is said to be of the cottage type and nowhere is the word "bungalow" used. However, the plan type had its origins in the Spanish or Mexican hacienda with living rooms across the front and courtyard access to rooms in the wings. The piers of the Craftsman porch were to be tree trunks for a rustic effect. One Craftsman detail not derived from Greene and Greene is the large number of fireplaces; each room had one. The cost of the house was estimated to be $2,000; thus it would be an inexpensive summer house.[6] In March 1905, the Craftsman house of the month (plate 50), called a bungalow, had a related L plan with veranda along the wings. Like the earlier courtyard house this one had tree-trunk piers. Even though this house was to be built of fieldstone, not a typical California bungalow material for an entire house, it seems closely linked to hacienda-type California bungalows. Perhaps Stickley was trying to acclimate the California bungalow to other areas of the United States.

48, 49. "Cool and Quiet Days," exterior and floor plan. *The Craftsman* 6, no. 4 (July 1904): following 402; 405.

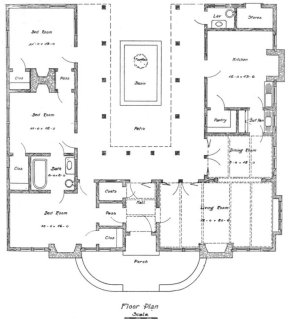

50. Craftsman bungalow, number three, series of 1905, exterior. *The Craftsman* 7, no. 6 (March 1905): following 736.

The California influence was acknowledged in the text of one of the January 1909 Craftsman houses (plate 51). The accompanying text suggested:

Such a plan would serve admirably for a dwelling in California or in the Southern States, but would be advisable only for specially favored spots in the North and East, as its comfort and charm necessarily depend very largely upon the possibility of outdoor life.[7]

Although this house does not seem to be a direct copy of a California house and could be called a bungalow only by stretching the term to include houses

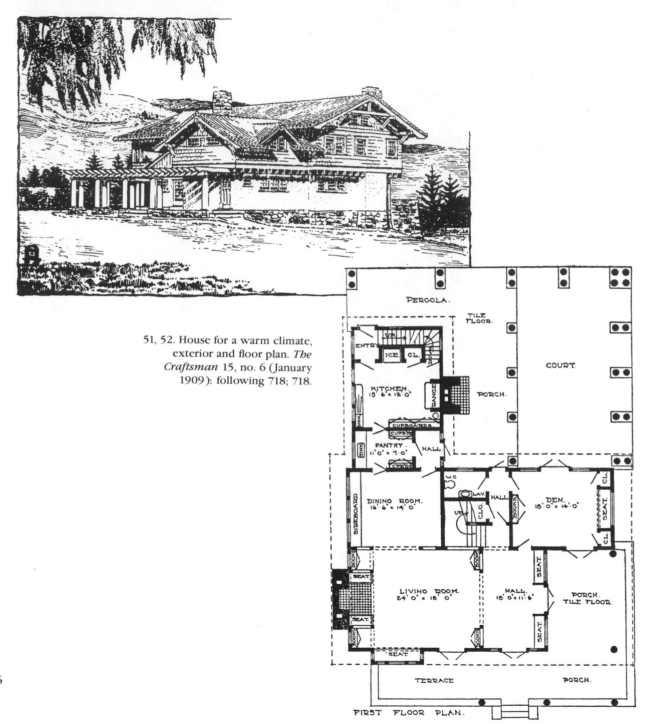

51, 52. House for a warm climate, exterior and floor plan. *The Craftsman* 15, no. 6 (January 1909): following 718; 718.

PERGOLA.

TILE FLOOR.

COURT.

ENTRY

ICE. CL.

KITCHEN.
15'·6" x 12'·0"

PORCH.

CUPBOARDS.
CUPB'D

PANTRY
11'·0" x 7'·0"

HALL.

W.C

LAV.

CLO.

HALL

DEN.
18'·0" x 14'·0"

CL.

SEAT.

CL.

DINING ROOM.
16'·6" x 14'·0"

SIDEBOARD

BOOKS

SEAT.

SEAT.

LIVING ROOM.
24'·0" x 18'·0"

HALL.
18'·0" x 11'·6"

SEAT.

PORCH.
TILE FLOOR.

SEAT.

SEAT.

SEAT.

TERRACE

PORCH.

FIRST FLOOR PLAN.

with two full stories, there is a general feeling of Greene and Greene influence in such exterior details as the boldly exposed wood beams and the pergolas, balconies, terraces, and porches which extend living space into the out-of-doors. When this house was published the first of the *Craftsman* articles on Greene and Greene had already appeared. Una Nixon Hopkins who often wrote *Craftsman* articles on California architecture had noted a distinct Craftsman house type in California, which was said to be entirely separate from the bungalow and adobe mission house forms; this California Craftsman house was distinguished by its sloping roof line, broad verandas, overhanging eaves, and rustic details.[8] The description generally fits houses by the Greene brothers as well as it does this Craftsman house. The ground floor plan (plate 52) shows the openness of the hall, living room, and dining room; however, the rear porch and court which could have served as useful extensions of the house are not closely connected to the main living areas. The same defect occurs on the second story where only hallways face the court.

Although *The Craftsman* contained frequent articles on California houses, its own Craftsman homes were not usually of the California type. The small Craftsman house tended to have a story and a half with bedrooms on the upper story under a steeply pitched roof with either dormer windows or a sleeping porch on the front side of the house. There were many variations on this theme. One cottage of this type (plates 53 and 54) was published in March 1909,[9] and built at least three times from free plans available to members of the Craftsman Home Builders' Club. The W. T. Johnson house (plate 55) in Lyons, New York[10] is closest to the published plan. The Johnson house, situated on a high ridge, has a fine view from the wide front porch. The exterior, originally covered with cypress shingles weathered to a silvery color, is now covered with shingles stained a dark brown. One change from the published house is the latticed gable ends of the front porch, an improvement which gives the porch an airy spaciousness and exposes the beams of the ceiling (plate 56).

The blueprints for the house are reversed so that the entrance is on the right. The chestnut-paneled living room, open to the entrance hall, stretches twenty-five feet across the front of the house. The inglenook with its typically Craftsman, built-in seat on one side has a wide fieldstone fireplace with a recessed niche over the opening (plate 57). For a house of its modest square footage, it has a remarkably large living room which seems even larger because the dining room is open to it. Craftsman electric fixtures with hammered amber glass were used throughout the first floor (plates 58 and 59).

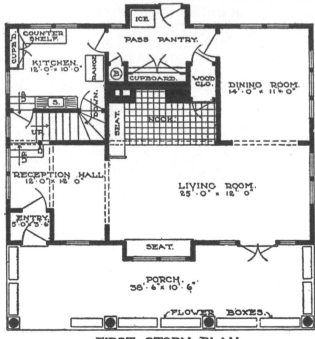

53, 54. Craftsman farmhouse, exterior and floor plan. *The Craftsman* 15, no. 6 (March 1909): following 718.

FIRST STORY PLAN

55, 56. W. T. Johnson house, Lyons, New
York, c. 1912, exterior and porch detail.
Photographs by Courtney Frisse.

57. W. T. Johnson house, Lyons, New York, c. 1912, inglenook. Photograph by Courtney Frisse.

58, 59. W. T. Johnson house, Lyons, New York, c. 1912, light fixtures. Photographs courtesy of Roger Cook.

The plan of the second story was changed somewhat to accommodate a fourth bedroom. The rear side was raised to include a long dormer. The dormer sleeping porch over the front porch is large enough to hold a double and a single bed. Stickley, along with others of his time, was a proponent of sleeping porches which are included in many of the Craftsman houses.

The Hugh Bonney house (plate 60) in Norwich, New York, a surprising variation of the same plan, illustrates just how much some Craftsman readers changed the Home Builders' Club plans. The exterior has no resemblance to the published plan. Judge Bonney stretched the ground floor plan at each end for a wider entrance hall, living room, and dining room and

60, 61. Hugh Bonney house, Norwich, New York, c. 1909, exterior and inglenook. Photographs courtesy of Terry Shorter.

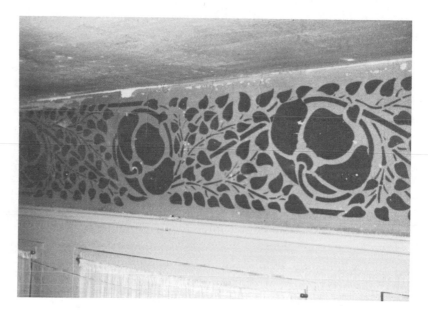

62. Hugh Bonney House, Norwich, New York, c. 1909, frieze.

turned a one-and-a-half-story plan into two full stories. His house also had an extended rear kitchen wing with a large sleeping porch above.

The first story interior, however, is close to the published house. Chestnut was used for paneling, moldings, and the built-in cabinets and seats which stretch across the entire front of the living room. The inglenook (plate 61) has a high-backed, built-in seat on one side and a wide brick fireplace. Unlike the Johnson house, the Bonney house does not have exposed ceiling beams. Craftsman light fixtures and door hardware were used throughout the house.

A recent remodeling of an upstairs bedroom in the Bonney house has revealed another characteristic Craftsman feature, a stenciled frieze of large flowers and leaves (plate 62) which seems to have been inspired by Art Nouveau designs. Similar stenciled frieze designs were often illustrated in

The Craftsman, and the typical Craftsman house could easily accommodate them. It would not be surprising if additional friezes were discovered in the Bonney house.

The Raymond Riordon house (plate 63) in Rolling Prairie, Indiana, is an adaptation of a Craftsman house published in 1910 as Craftsman house, number 93 (plate 64). This house is especially interesting because it was adapted for a specialized use and for a sloping site by George W. Maher (1864–1926), a member of the Chicago school. Maher had apprenticed in the Chicago office of Joseph Lyman Silsbee when Frank Lloyd Wright and George Grant Elmslie were also working there.[11] Thus some Chicago school influence might be expected in his adaptation; however, the house is very much of the Craftsman mode. Maher essentially raised the second floor and added long dormers on the front and back to provide more light and headroom for the second-story living room which Mr. Riordon, superintendent of the Interlaken School, needed as a large meeting place for his boarding students. The house was nestled into a hillside sloping down to a lake; therefore a retaining wall and court were built behind the house. The descriptive article on the Riordon house captured its essence and indeed the essence of the Craftsman house:

> Whether you view it from the lake, the garden or the clover-covered hillside, or whether you step inside its sheltered porch and hospitable rooms, you feel instinctively that it is a real home, planned by those who knew by heart the country, the materials and the needs of the people who were to live therein, and who have studied out, thoughtfully and lovingly, how to make the building fulfill those needs in the wisest and most beautiful way.[12]

The Craftsman house was a real home. Those people lucky enough to live in Craftsman houses now, years after they were built, feel that their houses are indeed homes in the best sense of the word.

Not all Craftsman homes were shingled. Many designs for concrete or stuccoed houses were published, usually with the note that other materials could be substituted to suit local conditions or personal tastes. In 1913–14, a cement-covered Craftsman house was built for Mr. and Mrs. Chauncey O. Garritt (plate 65) in Wellesley Hills, Massachusetts, as a wedding gift from Mrs. Garritt's father.[13] The house was meant to be fireproof with steel-beam construction and hollow block walls covered in rough-finished cement. Its design

63. Raymond Riordon house, Rolling Prairie, Indiana, exterior. *The Craftsman* 25, no. 1 (October 1913): following 48.

64. Craftsman house, number ninety-three, exterior. *The Craftsman* 18, no. 4 (July 10): 482.

had originally been published in *The Craftsman* in 1912,[14] with Gustav Stickley listed as architect.

In common with many other Craftsman houses which were built in newly developed residential areas, the Garritt house was constructed in Abbot Road Belevdere, a planned area with winding roads and ample building sites. The house plan (plate 66) is typically Craftsman with a large porch, open ground floor living space, and bedrooms fitted under a steeply sloping roof. The house was built with only minor changes from the published plan; a bay window with built-in seat was added to the living room, and a built-in cabinet was added to the dining room, taking some space away from the pantry. The fireplace is faced with tree-patterned Grueby tiles, a material Stickley had used in his own home and one often suggested to *Craftsman* readers. This and several other Craftsman houses have central vacuum cleaning systems with outlets leading to a robotlike motor in the basement. The second-story sleeping porch has been enclosed and a wing was added to the house in the 1920s.

Even though Stickley encouraged readers to make their own modifications to Craftsman plans, would-be Craftsman homeowners could also have plans adapted to their needs by the Craftsman staff. Mr. and Mrs. I. R. Williams of Ossining, New York, approached the Craftsman architects with a request for an adaptation of a plan published in May 1911 (plates 67 and 68).[15] Mrs. Williams was a dedicated *Craftsman* reader who felt that she had to have a real Craftsman house when the time came for the family to build on a newly opened street in Ossining. The Williams selected the floor plan they liked, but Mrs. Williams is said to have taken scissors in hand and cut through it to enlarge the house with space for an additional bedroom and bath to the right of the living room.

Since drawings of the various stages in the planning process still exist, it is possible to see how the designers and owners went about changing the exterior. First, a facade with a gabled front porch on the right was proposed (plate 69). Finally the gabled porch was moved to the left (plate 70). The use of a gabled porch rather than the porch which stretches across the facade of the published exterior makes a radical difference in appearance. Wood shingles and darkly painted woodwork were used as recommended.

The interior, originally furnished with Craftsman pieces, has wall surfaces divided by flat molding strips of fumed oak (plate 71), a treatment used for bedrooms in Stickley's house ten years earlier. The living room fireplace was constructed with a heating and ventilation system invented by Stickley

65. Chauncey O. Garritt House, Wellesley Hills, Massachusetts, 1913–14, exterior.
Photograph by Mary Ann Smith.

66. Craftsman cement house,
number 149, floor plan. *The
Craftsman* 23, no. 3 (December
1912): 336.

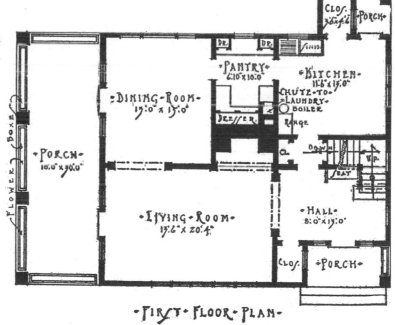

·FIRST·FLOOR·PLAN·

97

67, 68. Craftsman house, number 116, exterior and floor plan. *The Craftsman* 20, no. 2 (May 1911): 202, 203.

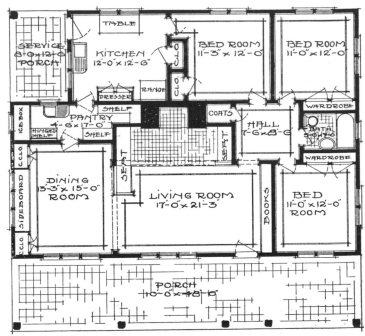

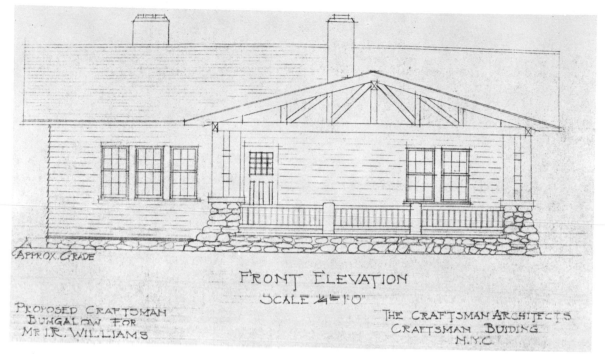

FRONT ELEVATION
SCALE ¼"=1'0"

PROPOSED CRAFTSMAN
BUNGALOW FOR
Mr I.R. WILLIAMS

THE CRAFTSMAN ARCHITECTS
CRAFTSMAN BUILDING
N.Y.C

69. I. R. Williams house, c. 1911, proposed elevation. Avery Architectural and Fine Arts Library, Columbia University.

70. I. R. Williams house, Ossining, New York, c. 1911, exterior. Photograph by Mary Ann Smith.

71, 72. I. R. Williams house, Ossining, New York, c. 1911, dining room and living room fireplace. Photographs by Fran Davies.

(plate 72).[16] The Craftsman fireplace system, built of iron and available for purchase, brought fresh air into the fireplace where it was warmed and circulated into the room through grills near the floor and close to the ceiling. In the Williams house a grilled opening into a bedroom behind the fireplace allowed warm air to circulate there as well. The Craftsman fireplace, said to be efficient enough to heat an entire small house, apparently did heat the Williams house through most of the winter.

Dumblane (plate 73), one of the finest of all Craftsman houses and also one of the largest, was another adaptation of a Craftsman plan by the Craftsman architects.[17] It was built in Washington, D.C., in 1912, by Mr. and Mrs. S. Hazen Bond. Mr. Bond, a prominent Washington attorney who had an intense interest in his home, built much of the furniture from *Craftsman* designs. He was so proud of Dumblane that he even published two booklets based on the *Craftsman* article, presumably to give to his friends. He had much to be proud of in Dumblane.

The site of Dumblane, the highest point in the District of Columbia, overlooked the Potomac Valley with the Blue Ridge Mountains in the distance. When Dumblane was built the surrounding area was still semirural; unfortunately much of the site was later sold and now houses stand close to Dumblane, obstructing the view from its long porch.

The design of Dumblane was based on a 1904 Craftsman house design (plate 74).[18] The facade gable of the 1904 design was eliminated, and a number of minor changes were made in the floor plans, most of which had to do with enlarging rooms. The Dumblane plans (plates 75 and 76) are an improvement over the original Craftsman plans in that they provide for a dining porch, larger entrance hall, and grander staircase.

Dumblane is approached from a rear corner of the property. After passing the garage, an almost Craftsman house in miniature where Mr. Bond built furniture, a visitor walks through the pergola (plate 77) at the side of the house and along the front porch to the main entrance. Thus the exterior is experienced close to the house rather than from some distant point of view. This was always the sequence of entrance to Dumblane, and it is unusual for a Craftsman house which generally would be approached from a front walkway.

Mr. Bond, who supervised the construction, obviously meant for Dumblane to remain standing for a long time. Above concrete foundations, the eighteen-inch-thick outer walls are built of brick, and the nine-inch partition walls are reinforced with steel columns. Huge, rough-textured tapestry bricks,

73. Dumblane, S. Hazen Bond house, Washington, D.C., 1912, exterior. *The Craftsman* 23, no. 5 (February 1913): following 522.

74. Craftsman house, number ten, series of 1904, exterior. *The Craftsman* 7, no. 1 (October 1904): following p. 76.

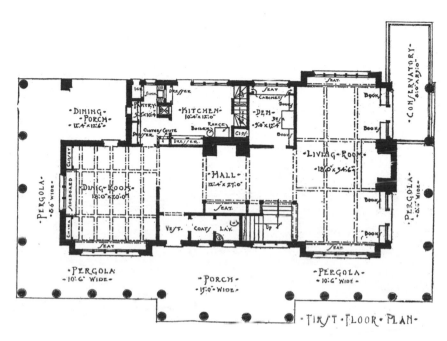

·FIRST·FLOOR·PLAN·

75, 76. Dumblane, S. Hazen Bond house, Washington, D.C.,
1912, first and second floor plans. *The Craftsman* 23, no. 5
(February 1913): 533, 534.

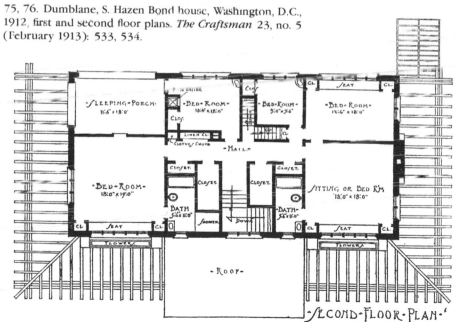

·SECOND·FLOOR·PLAN·

77. Dumblane, S. Hazen Bond house, Washington, D.C., 1912, pergola. Photograph by Mary Ann Smith.

$12'' \times 4'' \times 2''$ of varied colors from salmon pink to dark blue were used for the exterior; these ten pound bricks were set in thick mortar joints which project slightly for a rough-textured effect. The blue green roof tiles and oiled cypress woodwork were chosen to harmonize with the brick. Craftsman light fixtures were used throughout the house.

Mr. Bond must have liked modern conveniences. His house had a hoist for raising ashes from the basement, a cold storage pit, an elevator to carry coal from the basement to the fireplaces, and a turbine central vacuum cleaner. The family cats had basement cages connected to outdoor cages by pipes.

A sixty-five-foot axis continues from the living room through the entrance hall to the dining room. The entrance hall, a large room in itself, has a fireplace with a copper hood carrying the house motto, "Each man's chimney is

78. Dumblane, S. Hazen Bond house, Washington, D.C., 1912, hall. "Dumblane, The Suburban Estate of S. Hazen Bond," n.d.

his golden milestone." Opposite is the hall seat (plate 78), under which was the nine-foot room for an electric "talking machine." The curve above the built in seat, as the *Craftsman* article was careful to note, is "the only curve used in the construction."[19]

The dining room and living room were carefully furnished with Craftsman wicker and oak furniture stained to match the woodwork (plate 79); some of the furniture was custom-made by the Craftsman Workshops to Mr. Bond's designs. Even the china and silverware were made to order to complement the luxurious simplicity of the house. Mrs. Bond made the curtains and pillow covers from Craftsman designs. This was the perfect Craftsman house resulting from the involvement of the owners at every stage of planning and execution, Mr. Bond making furniture and finishing woodwork, Mrs. Bond planting gardens and sewing for the house. Although

79. Dumblane, S. Hazen Bond house, Washington, D.C., 1912, living room. *The Craftsman* 23, no. 5 (February 1913): following 528.

Dumblane was considerably larger and more costly than most Craftsman homes and so not typical, it represents the values Gustav Stickley espoused in his magazine.

The *Craftsman* reader, equipped with a free set of plans or plans personally adapted by the Craftsman architects, had a good chance of building a house which conformed to Stickley's ideals of middle-class comfort, wholesome family life, and structural simplicity. Although the Craftsman house designs varied in size and quality, most of them embodied those often-expressed Craftsman qualities which Stickley was so fond of enumerating.

The Craftsman house was never cheap to build. In 1910, Stickley even cautioned readers that Craftsman houses might cost more than other houses of their size because of the special materials and workmanship necessary for the harmonious whole.[20] The Craftsman house in all its forms was, however, the perfect setting for Craftsman furniture and a fine setting for American life.

6

OTHER CRAFTSMAN HOUSES

USTAV STICKLEY'S CRAFTSMAN DESIGNERS planned custom houses in addition to distributing Craftsman plans to readers and modifying published plans to suit individual needs; for about a year Stickley even built houses in the northeastern United States. Stickley probably saw the Craftsman house as the logical extension of his furniture manufacturing, and he seems to have enjoyed building houses as an activity uniting all his Arts and Crafts interests. Here he was following the example set by William Morris so many years earlier.

In 1905, Stickley moved to New York City, where he established a new Craftsman showroom and publishing offices at 29 West Thirty-fourth Street. He probably made this major move in hopes of reaching a wider clientele for his Craftsman products. He had to find a new headquarters because the Crouse Stables which housed his Craftsman offices and showrooms was sold at this time; perhaps the necessity of moving to new headquarters was a deciding factor in his transfer of operations to New York City. At first, Stickley lived in a New York apartment[1] and returned to Syracuse periodically to visit his family and his Eastwood factory. However, he had long dreamed of establishing a cooperative community where families would produce their own food and various crafts in their homes. As early as 1904 while visiting California, he thought he saw the ideal location for such a community in Palm Valley.[2] Although he quickly decided the California location was inadequate, he continued to dream of a community of like-minded workers.

In 1908, he purchased a large plot of land in Morris Plains, New Jersey, and announced to *Craftsman* readers that he intended to build a new home there together with a school:

> for the definite working out of the theory I have so long held of reviving practical and profitable handicrafts in connection with small farming carried out by modern methods of intensive agriculture.[3]

80. Proposed Gustav Stickley house, Craftsman Farms, Morris Plains, New Jersey, 1908, exterior. *The Craftsman* 15, no. 1 (October 1908): following 80.

The idea of a school was an outgrowth of his earlier interest in a cooperative community. Quite naturally, the house he proposed to build at Craftsman Farms (plate 80) was to be an exemplar of Craftsman ideals; although this first house was not built, its plan was the basis of the Stickley home eventually contructed at Craftsman Farms. There were three design requirements for the house; it must be exactly suited to the life lived in it; it should harmonize with the environment; its materials, as far as possible, should be from the site and left in their natural condition. Therefore, he planned to use native fieldstone for the foundation and lower walls and chestnut logs for the exposed timbers. The upper walls, built of hollow tiles, were to be rough plastered and ornamented with large tile panels appropriately illustrating various farm activities; the chestnut logs were to be used structurally with the outer surfaces left rounded and stained in a gray brown tone to resemble bark. Pergolas of red cedar logs were planned for the front of the house and the side, where an outdoor dining room and cooking fireplace were to be located. The pergolas and other links to the surroundings emphasized the country setting.[4] The number of structural details included in the *Craftsman* article on this proposed house indicates that Stickley was serious about constructing it. However, there was an evolution of plans before he finally built his Craftsman Farms house.

Soon Stickley announced that since the first necessity for Craftsman Farms was a clubhouse for meetings, lectures, and entertainment, construction of such a building would begin in the spring of 1909. The proposed clubhouse was to be built in place of the house he had proposed earlier. Log construction would be used since chestnut trees were readily available on the property and therefore the least expensive building material.[5] He liked log houses because of their primitiveness, simplicity, and association with early American life; and he had published three Craftsman log houses in 1907.[6] The proposed clubhouse (plate 81), in common with a number of other Craftsman house designs, was to have a porch across the front and a wide dormer to illuminate second-story rooms. The gable ends were to have a log half-timbered structure similar to the house earlier proposed for the same site. The first floor plan (plate 82) was divided into three long sections: the porch, reception room, and kitchen-sitting room. Each section was articulated on the ends of the house by the round log ends of exterior walls and the center partition. The second story was to be used for guest rooms, a ladies' rest room, and two additional bathrooms. The basement was to contain a smoking room and men's rest room. Thus there was a three-part horizontal division of the clubhouse—for women, joint activities, and men — as well as the three-part floor plan division. The clubhouse, like the first Stickley home planned for Craftsman Farms, was never built; its plan, however, acted as an intermediary step to the house finally built on the site.

The building which became Stickley's Craftsman Farms home was originally planned as a clubhouse; its use as the Stickley home was considered only temporary. Mrs. Stickley and the Stickley children moved from Syracuse to Morris Plains in July 1910, after the family furniture and pet dog were safely installed there.[7] Since their new log house was meant to be a clubhouse, adjustments were necessary for conversion to family life. The exterior (plate 83) resembles the earlier clubhouse, the major differences being the substitu-

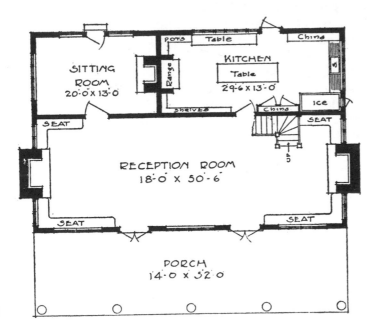

81, 82. Proposed clubhouse, Craftsman Farms, Morris Plains, New Jersey, 1908, exterior and first floor plan. *The Craftsman* 15, no. 3 (December 1908): following 340; 340.

83. Gustav Stickley house, Craftsman Farms, Morris Plains, New Jersey, 1910, exterior. *The Craftsman* 21, no. 2 (November 1911): following 196.

tion of shingles for the half-timbering of the gable, the raising of the long front dormer, and the addition of an identical rear dormer. A rear kitchen wing was added so that the portion originally planned as a kitchen-sitting room became a long dining room. A first floor plan of December 1908 (plate 84) is marked with penciled changes in the location of the staircase and fireplaces dividing the kitchen and sitting room which became one room with the fireplaces eliminated. The second story was changed more radically into family bedrooms.

A laudatory description of Stickley's new house appeared in *The*

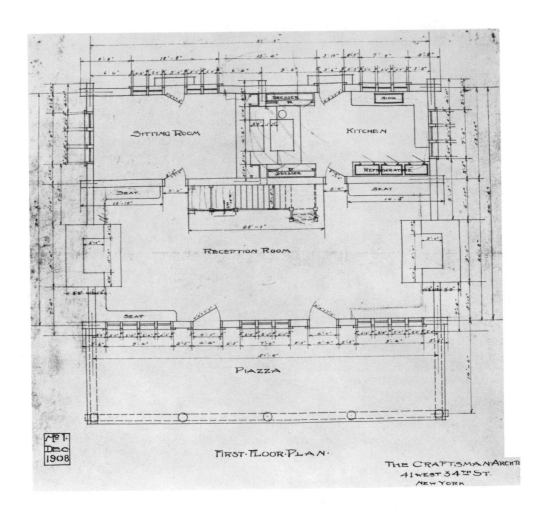

84. Gustav Stickley house, Craftsman Farms, Morris Plains, New Jersey, 1908, first floor plan. Avery Architectural and Fine Arts Library, Columbia University.

Craftsman in 1911. As might be expected, the simplicity of structure and the honesty of logs left uncovered were praised. Describing the large living room (plates 85 and 86), the author says:

85, 86. Gustav Stickley house, Craftsman Farms, Morris Plains, New Jersey, 1910, living room. *The Craftsman* 21, no. 2 (November 1911): following 196.

> There is something nobly barbaric in the massive rough-hewn posts supporting the stout beams overhead, the two great hearths with their copper hoods, the crude beauty of the natural wood and the glint of color of the dull orange hangings.[8]

Stickley's house even reminded the enthusiastic author of William Morris' poems, surely the greatest of praise!

Gustav Stickley must have been delighted with the Morris comparison although it seems a bit farfetched for an essentially American log house. The living room is impressive. At opposite ends of the fifty-foot-long room are massive stone fireplaces with Stickley's heat circulating system.[9] One of the large copper hoods bears a favorite Stickley maxim, "The lyf so short the craft so long to lerne" which appeared often in *The Craftsman*. Although the center ceiling timber is in reality three logs spliced together, it appears to be one log. The walls are made of stripped logs stained a bark color. Craftsman furniture, some of it probably from Stickley's Syracuse house, and distinctive Craftsman hanging lamps and hardware (plate 87) were used throughout the house.

Designers' homes are interesting because they illustrate individual tastes unhampered by the demands of clients. Gustav Stickley's Craftsman Farms house was a showcase of his interests in primitivism and country life. His involvement in farm life extended beyond the bounds of his log house to include orchards, gardens, and dairy cattle. He wanted to build a colony of small cottages, but his project never materialized fully. He did construct two small cottages, one of which was occupied by his daughter, Barbara, and her husband, Ben Wiles, who was business manager of *The Craftsman*.

Craftsman Farms was Gustav Stickley's idea of perfection and because it was so important to him, he wanted to share its beauties and its wholesomeness with others. He planned to establish a school there to teach boys between the ages of seven and sixteen to become useful citizens through cooperative experiences in farming and selling the fruits of their labor. He planned a program of study with Raymond Riordon, Superintendent of the Interlaken School in Rolling Prairie, Indiana. Like Stickley, Mr. Riordon had a Craftsman house as the center of his school. When Mr. Riordon visited Craftsman Farms, Stickley explained its importance to him:

> This is my Garden of Eden. This is the realization of the dreams that I

87. Gustav Stickley house, Craftsman Farms, Morris Plains, New Jersey, 1910, door hardware. Photograph courtesy of Roger Cook.

had when I worked as a lad. It is because my own dreams have come true that I want other boys to dream out their own good future here for themselves.[10]

117

Stickley's statement about his "Garden of Eden," his dream come true, is poignant and touching, especially so since the totality of his dream with his School for Citizenship did not come true. The school never opened.

Even though Stickley was never able to open his school at Craftsman Farms or to build all the cottages he had hoped to have there, he did gain useful experience in construction as he erected his own house and other farm structures. Earlier, he had published many house designs in *The Craftsman* and written about them. Now while planning his Craftsman Farms home, he saw his own designs actualized as real Craftsman architecture. In 1909, he moved to a new level of involvement in Craftsman houses; he organized the Craftsman House Building Company. Since he now lived within commuting distance of New York and had his main office there, his construction activities were confined to the greater New York area. The houses his company built are located in northern New Jersey and Long Island. His construction company was active for a short time, less than a year, and so he probably built only a small number of homes. Unfortunately the total number of these houses is unknown since his business records of the period are incomplete. Several of the houses were published in *The Craftsman* as "perfect expressions of the Craftsman idea" in designs, materials, and construction. These houses were thought to be of special interest to readers because they illustrated:

> how closely we have been able to adhere to the bold position we took in the beginning; a position that implied a radical departure from the style of architecture which prevailed even six or eight years ago, and one which we have been able to maintain and strengthen because of the straightforwardness and common sense of the idea it conveyed.[11]

The houses Stickley's company built are two story, shingled or stuccoed homes, usually with center entrance halls flanked on one side by the living room with a dining room or den on the other side. The interiors with their beautifully finished Craftsman woodwork are especially fine. The wood used by Stickley's workmen seems to have been of the same grade as his furniture wood and was even stamped as "Craftsman" on the end of the boards.[12]

The Frederick M. Hill house (plate 88) in Great Neck, New York is a good example of the custom built Craftsman home. A *Craftsman* article described the Hill house as having "a good deal of the quiet conservative dignity of the old Colonial farmhouse [because] the exterior shows not one superfluous feature and its beauty is entirely that of line and proportion and the impression it gives of simplicity."[13] This seems an appropriate description of the Hill house, originally covered with darkly stained shingles, now stuccoed. Its central entrance and symmetrical facade do recall the simple houses of the early eighteenth century. Built in a suburb of amply proportioned, solid houses of about the same date, the Hill house is noticeable because of its forthright exterior and rectilinear detailing which contrast with neighboring homes often embellished with neo-colonial detailing. The Hill house seems closer to the essence of the early American colonial house without the Georgian detailing meant to make a house look "colonial" in the twentieth century.

The openness of the ground floor plan (plate 89) of the Hill house recalls Stickley's Syracuse house as does the paneled wall treatment used in the living room, hall, and dining room (plate 90). As in Stickley's own houses in Syracuse and Morris Plains, interior doors have amber hammered glass panes.

In the same year, 1909, the Craftsman House Building Company also built a house for Dr. Mary Richards (plate 91) in nearby Garden City, Long Island, New York.[14] The article describing Dr. Richards' house was placed in the advertising section of *The Craftsman* as a promotion for the new construction company. Like so many other Craftsman houses, the Richards home was built in a new housing tract, near a five-hundred-acre area which had been opened about two years earlier. Stickley saw Garden City Estates as a good place to live:

> because we think the conditions therein are contributing to the expression of what we believe to be the ideal of home life, — large open spaces, plenty of air and light, detached houses and sunny gardens, which all help to promote the simple, neighborly relations of the country, — and at the same time, the urban advantages of fine roads, public and private, and perfect sanitation.[15]

The small entrance porch of Dr. Richards' half-timbered house is similar to the porch of the Hill house and others built by the company. In the true Craftsman fashion of honest structural expression, the joists supporting the

88, 89. Frederick M. Hill house, Great Neck, New York, 1909, exterior and first floor plan. *The Craftsman* 18, no. 6 (September 1910): following 662; 666.

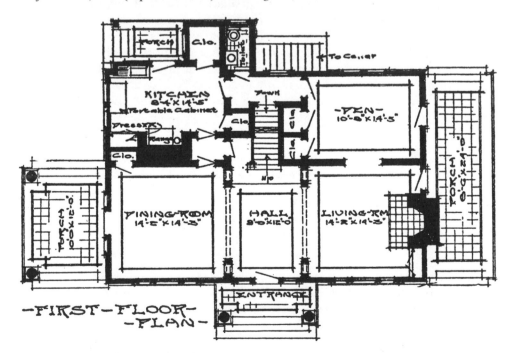

90. Frederick M. Hill house, Great Neck, New York, 1909, living room. *The Craftsman* 18, no. 6 (September 1910): following 666

second story of the Richards house project to the sides where they are left exposed. Because Mary Richards was a doctor, the first story of her house has an office on one side of the entrance hall. However, as the article was careful to point out, a hall was not usual in a Craftsman house, and here the living room was almost a part of the hall. This is a confusing statement since many Craftsman houses have halls and all the published houses built by the company in 1909 had hallways! Perhaps client demands conflicted with Craftsman philosophy.

Although the few houses constructed by the Craftsman House Building Company were attractive, sturdy, and very livable, this branch of Stickley's

91. Mary Richards house, Garden City, New York, 1909, exterior. Photograph by Mary Ann Smith.

enterprises seems to have been unsuccessful. It may be that the problems of construction in scattered locations, even within the greater New York area, were too great for the company to be profitable. After October 9, 1909, all receipt and disbursement records for the construction company terminated.[16]

The several houses constructed by Stickley's company stand as concrete examples of what Stickley's involvement with clients throughout the building process could accomplish. The interiors, as might be expected, are carefully planned and beautifully finished. The floor plans are quite practical for family life, and the exteriors are well crafted. The fairly large size of the houses, certainly grander than the many bungalows and cottages published in *The Craftsman,* and their locations in prosperous suburbs indicate that the *Craftsman* readers who wanted Stickley-built houses were probably from the upper middle class. These clients obviously believed in Stickley's approach to design and construction and rejected the more usual styles of the early twentieth century; however, they wanted substantial houses in good neighborhoods and could afford them. The simple country cottage so often advocated in *The Craftsman* was not for them. Thus there is a dichotomy between the Craftsman ideal of the simple life in the inexpensive house and the reality of the Craftsman-built house for the wealthier client. This does not mean that the people who commissioned Craftsman homes wanted ornate, elaborate residences but rather that they could afford the costs of handsomely executed simplicity.

The Craftsman Architects, unfortunately nameless, continued to design custom houses after the House Building Company went out of business. These designer-draftsmen were responsible for the finished drawings of houses published in *The Craftsman* and adaptations of published plans to individual needs as was the case with the Williams house in Ossining, New York, and Dumblane in Washington, D.C.[18] One of the published custom-designed Craftsman houses belonged to Mr. F. S. Peer (plate 92). Located in Ithaca, New York, the Peer house appeared in *The Craftsman* in 1913.[19] Gustav Stickley was listed as architect although the blueprints were signed by the Craftsman Architects, a clear indication of the relative roles Stickley and his employees played in the design. The Peer house design is closer to English Arts and Crafts architecture than most Craftsman houses, perhaps because the client was an Englishman. The white rough cast stucco, simple half-timbering, and small-paned windows are reminiscent of Baillie Scott and Voysey, but these details were also present in earlier Craftsman houses. The treatment of end chimneys (plate 93), integrated into the stuccoed exterior to the extent that they resemble projections of interior spaces rather than chimney stacks, is reminiscent of contemporary English architecture, but the long dormers are a common Craftsman detail used in earlier houses.

The published plans for the Peer house (plates 94 and 95) were changed considerably when it was built; the ground floor powder room and conservatory were eliminated as was the entire attic story. The porch which was meant to have a center pergola to allow light into the hall was completely roofed, making the rear stair hall rather dark. Although the Peer house conforms to the traditional formula of center hall flanked by living and dining rooms, the adaptation to the hilltop view by means of the long rear porch is admirable.

92. F. S. Peer house, Ithaca, New York, 1913, exterior. *The Craftsman* 24, no. 1 (April 1913): following 70.

93. F. S. Peer house, Ithaca, New York, 1913, chimney detail. Photograph by Mary Ann Smith.

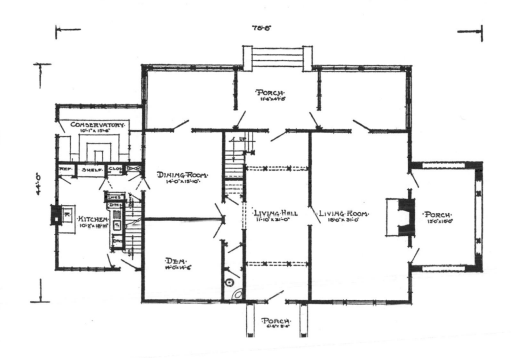

94, 95. F. S. Peer house, Ithaca, New York, 1913, first and second floor plans. *The Craftsman* 24, no. 1 (April 1913):69, 70.

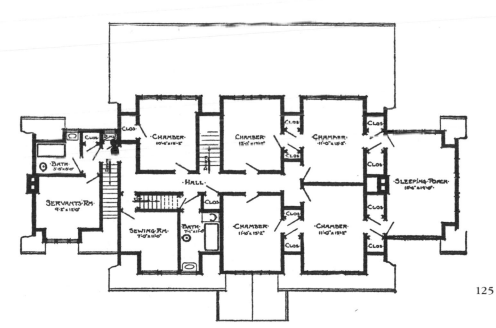

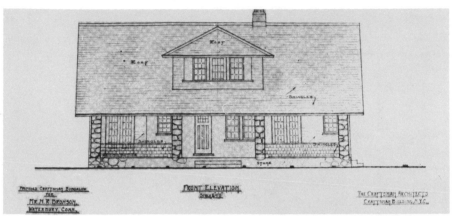

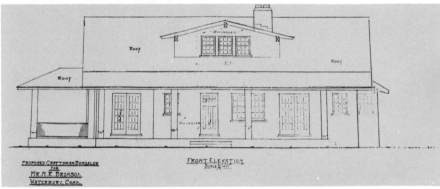

96, 97. Nathaniel R. Bronson house, Middlebury, Connecticut, 1914, elevation (top), and alternative elevation (bottom). Avery Architectural and Fine Arts Library, Columbia University.

Another of the custom-designed Craftsman houses, similar to many published houses in exterior appearance but with an unusual floor plan, was designed for Nathaniel R. Bronson in March 1914.[20] Mr. Bronson, a prominent attorney in Waterbury, Connecticut, and a member of a well-known local family, commissioned his rustic Craftsman house (plate 96) as a weekend retreat in Middlebury, a small community near Waterbury. In true Craftsman fashion the house exterior is darkly stained shingles. Since the house is sited on a hilltop, a porch stretches across the front, and the second floor sleeping porch has a fine view of the surrounding countryside. Several alternative elevations (plate 97) were done for Mr. Bronson, most of them concerned with various treatments of the porches. Although the Bronson house exterior is similar to that of the Johnson house[21] in Lyons, New York, the floor plans are quite different. To provide for an uninterrupted living-dining room space across the front of the house, the staircase of the Bronson house was relegated to the rear.

The Charles B. Evans house (plate 98) in Douglaston, Long Island, New York, does not resemble other Craftsman houses although it was also designed in 1914 by the Craftsman architects.[22] The brick Tudor arch of the entrance and the eyebrow window in the tiled roof are details which were also used in nearby houses. The fact that the exterior is so similar to its neighbors suggests that by 1914 Gustav Stickley was finding compromise necessary in Craftsman house designs. Perhaps the Evans family felt it was important that their house blend into the neighborhood.

The interior of the Evans house, however, is distinctly Craftsman. The Craftsman light fixtures and much of the Craftsman furniture purchased by the family when the house was new are still intact. The use of board woodwork to define wall areas structurally continues the Craftsman tradition as does the fumed finish of woodwork to match the furniture. Like the Hill house (plates 88, 89 and 90), the Evans house has a center hall plan with living room and dining room very open to the hall so that the forty-three-foot length of the house is immediately discernible (plates 99, 100, and 101). Since the ceiling beams of the living room do not continue through the hall and into the dining room in a straight line, the visual continuity is somewhat broken although the rooms form an almost completely open space. The staircase (plate 102) has a pierced board hand railing similar to the design Stickley had used in his house at Craftsman Farms.

Several characteristics of Stickley's approach to house design are apparent in the Evans house. First, like other large Craftsman houses, the Evans house has a symmetrical facade with center entrance, a design formula originating in the earliest of American eighteenth-century homes. Second, the floor plan has a center stair hall flanked by living and dining rooms. Third, and surely the most interesting feature of this house, it has a typical Craftsman interior of the type developed more than ten years earlier in Stickley's Syracuse house. The typical Craftsman interior door design, tapestry brick fireplace, and light fixtures used in the Evans house had all been designed years

98, 99. Charles B. Evans house, Douglaston, New York, 1914, exterior and living room. Photographs by Mary Ann Smith.

100, 101. Charles B. Evans house, Douglaston, New York, 1914, entrance hall and dining room. Plate 100 photographs by Mary Ann Smith; plate 101 photograph by Rick Echelmeyer, courtesy of The Artsman, Bryn Mawr, Pennsylvania.

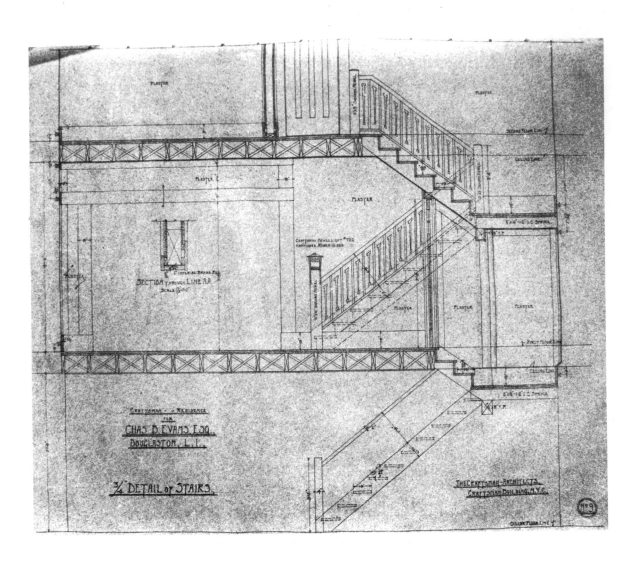

102. Charles B. Evans house, Douglaston, New York, 1914, stair detail. Avery Architectural and Fine Arts Library, Columbia University.

earlier. These details give a distinctiveness to Craftsman interiors and make it very easy to identify Craftsman houses regardless of differences in external appearances. It is not surprising that these details were used in so many Craftsman houses since Stickley obviously felt that he had designed the ideal interior; if this were so, there was no reason to change interior designs. The Evans house with its interior articulation of structure is a natural descendant of all earlier Craftsman homes.

The Craftsman house, as much as Craftsman furniture and *The Craftsman* magazine, expressed Gustav Stickley's design philosophy. If such were not the case, he would not have spent so much of his time in its development. His Craftsman Farms was an attempt to realize a childhood dream of country life in a log house. The Craftsman House Building Company briefly attempted to construct the ideal house; even after the building company ceased building, the Craftsman architects continued to design custom houses which combined a client's tastes with tried and true Craftsman ideas. Fortunately a number of the houses resulting from Stickley's various involvements still stand to inform us of his Craftsman ideals.

7

THE CRAFTSMAN, RECOGNITION OF ARCHITECTS, AND PLANNING

URING ALL THOSE YEARS when Stickley was publishing house plans in *The Craftsman* and he and the Craftsman architects were designing custom houses or revising published ones, his magazine also featured designs by other architects and sometimes articles by the architects themselves to explain their work. In some cases he recognized the talents of architects before their work became more generally known. Since his interests extended beyond the scope of the single house to the design of new towns and garden suburbs, *The Craftsman* also contained information on urban planning.

While most *Craftsman* architectural articles concerned houses, a series on the appropriate style for commercial and public buildings emerged in *The Craftsman* in 1905. The series began with an article by architect Frederick Stymetz Lamb (1863–1928), "Modern Use of the Gothic: The Possibilities of a New Architectural Style," in which a continuing discussion was invited. Lamb discounted Classicism and the Renaissance as design models and proposed the Gothic for asymmetrically planned buildings and the skyscraper.[1]

Lamb's article had the desired result of stimulating comment from other architects. Professor Alfred Dwight Foster Hamlin (1855–1926), executive head of Columbia University's School of Architecture, began his reply with an analysis of the structural and aesthetic aspects of "style." He felt that Gothic forms were appropriate to many building types and prophesized that eclecticism would mark the progress of twentieth-century design. Hamlin did have the good sense to praise Daniel Burnham and Louis Sullivan for their contributions to office building design.[2] Bertran C. Goodhue (1869–1924), a partner in the firm of Cram, Goodhue and Ferguson, contributed a short essay suggesting that there would probably never again be a distinctive style.[3] Samuel Howe who had earlier written a *Craftsman* article about Stickley's house joined the discussion by recommending that architects study the "constructive" approach of the Gothic period.[4] Thus far the discussion was rather tame and conservative.

If the discussion had ended at this point with general agreement on the appropriateness of the Gothic style for twentieth-century architecture, the "architectural discussion" would be unworthy of note. However, the next architect to enter the discussion was Louis Sullivan (1856–1924). He attacked the use of the Classic and Gothic styles:

> The flaw in our current architectural reasoning (if reasoning it may be called) lies in the fact (curious enough, to the logical mind), of a persistence in refusing to discriminate between *was* and *is;* and this, —in open view of the clear truth that nature, which surrounds us with its life,—always thus discriminates with precision. Hence with each discussion comes merely an added and ever-futile attempt to detach an art from the civilization which gave it birth....
>
> Corruption has gone so far, that it is time for a reaction. Not a trivial reaction from Classic to Gothic; but a fundamental reaction from irresponsibility to responsibility; from irrational to rational ideas; from confused to clear thinking. It is time for the nightmare of our feudalism to end, and for us to awaken to the reality of healthful life....
>
> Therefore is all special pleading for Classic, Gothic, or any other "ic" or "ance," irrelevant, immaterial and inconsequential.
>
> What is of consequence, is vital direct thinking stripped of all hypocrisy, pedantry and dilettantism.
>
> Our need is for fresh air and a general mental sanitation.[5]

In the next issue of *The Craftsman* Louis Sullivan's "Form and Function Artistically Considered" was published with an editor's note which quoted a letter from Sullivan to Stickley:

> I like the Spirit you are infusing into *The Craftsman.* It comes at a critical time—a time of ferment, a time of epoch-making changes. I hope you have the courage to see and grasp the opportunity to draw out opinion on issue, believing that you realize how noble a system of design (architectural thinking) might be founded upon the superb underlying qualities of the American people,—a people in whom I have a profound faith, in spite of our temporary insanity. America has long owed the world a new and sane philosophy, in gratitude for that liberty of mind which centuries of struggle have prepared for it.[6]

Sullivan's article, a slightly condensed reprint of "The Tall Office Building Artistically Considered" originally published in *Lippincott's Magazine* 57 (March 1896), is his analysis of the design of the skyscraper with exterior articulation according to the functions of the various floors. Here Sullivan's famous dictum appears italicized for emphasis: *form ever follows function. This is the law.*[7]

Thus the "architectural discussion" which enlivened *The Craftsman* provided Louis Sullivan with a forum for his opinions. The publication of a three-part Sullivan article in May through July 1906, "What Is Architecture? A Study of the American People Today," gave Sullivan another chance to make his ideas known. Carl K. Bennett, a bank officer, was so impressed by Sullivan's *Craftsman* three-part article that he commissioned the architect to design the National Farmers' Bank in Owatonna, Minnesota.[8] Although it is sometimes difficult to trace direct influences from magazine articles, here the result of the Sullivan *Craftsman* pieces is certain.

Sullivan's "Form follows function" dictum and his protest against the use of Classical and Gothic forms were echoed seven years later by two well-known architects, William Gray Purcell (1880–1965) and George Grant Elmslie (1871–1952) in another *Craftsman* article. It is hardly surprising that Purcell and Elmslie would echo Sullivan's beliefs since they had worked for him before forming their partnership. They rightly suggested that the tall office building was the true American architecture which would be regarded on its own merits in the future.[9] Their analysis of skyscraper articulation replicates Sullivan's, and their functionalist doctrine, italicized like Sullivan's for emphasis, *"When use does not change, form does not change"*[10] is a paraphrase of "Form follows function."

Aside from the several *Craftsman* articles by Louis Sullivan and the single piece by Purcell and Elmslie, Stickley ignored the Chicago school of architecture. This seems surprising since the distinctive Prairie houses Frank Lloyd Wright and others were developing were based in part on Arts and Crafts principles. Stickley could not have been unaware of midwestern prairie houses since they were published in a number of magazines. Moreover, he had other midwestern connections besides Sullivan, Purcell, and Elmslie. For example, Oscar Lovell Triggs who wrote four *Craftsman* articles was a founder and leader of the Industrial Arts League of Chicago, an organization related in spirit to the Chicago Arts and Crafts Society whose charter members included Myron Hunt, Dwight Perkins, Robert Spencer, and Frank Lloyd

135

103. Cottage, Wilson Eyre, Great Neck, Long Island, New York, front elevation. *The Craftsman* 3, no. 1 (October 1902): following 128.

Wright.[11] Certainly the Arts and Crafts Movement was vigorous in Chicago at just the time Stickley was beginning *The Craftsman*. In fact, *The House Beautiful,* a rival magazine based in Chicago, had contained some of the earliest illustrations of Stickley's furniture.[12] There is no indication in *The Craftsman* that Stickley disapproved of the Chicago school; he simply did not recognize it in his magazine.

Stickley did have the insight to recognize the eastern architect Wilson Eyre (1858–1944), whose work appeared several times in *The Craftsman*. As early as 1902, an anonymous article was illustrated with Eyre houses inspired by the English Arts and Crafts Movement (plate 103). Eyre was called a pioneer in American domestic architecture in a 1909 *Craftsman* article which compared his houses to those of English villages in their use of local materials. The author felt that the beauty of Eyre's architecture grew "out of the thoroughness with which the constructive problems are solved, and the necessary work is done."[13] A few months later another analysis of Eyre's work appeared; again, the English influence on his work was noted as was his honesty of construction and restrained use of ornamentation. His unusually close attention to the design of interiors was cited as a mark of his excellence.[14] These were qualities which would appeal to Stickley.

Wilson Eyre wrote an article for *The Craftsman* in 1913, using his own houses and several by other architects to illustrate what he considered to be American achievements in house design. He felt that successful American houses could only be designed by adaptation of "old ideals to new conditions." He was conscious of American innovations in house design such as the porches, verandas, and pergolas needed for outdoor life and the compact arrangements of hallways, kitchens, and service areas.[15] Stickley would surely have agreed with Eyre on the advisability of adaptation of the old to the new and the use of porches to link the interior with the surroundings of a house.

Although Stickley largely ignored midwestern architecture, he devoted many pages of *The Craftsman* to California architects. In general he admired the adaptation to climate, honest use of materials, and simplicity of California houses. *The Craftsman* singled out the Greene brothers of Pasadena for special attention in several articles. Charles and Henry Greene had all the architectural qualities Stickley admired. Their respect for good craftsmanship and their love of wood as a building material probably originated in the manual arts high school they had attended in St. Louis. They were concerned, like Stickley, with every aspect of house design from the house form to hardware, light fixtures, and furniture.

Greene and Greene houses appeared in a 1907 *Craftsman* article as examples of the Japanese influence on American architecture. Such details as the low pitched roof and exposed beams of Charles Greene's own house, begun in 1901, and the Theodore Irwin house (plate 104), enlarged in 1906, illustrate the article. However, it was the relationship of the houses to their irregular sites which pleased the author most. What could have been a problem was turned to an advantage through the use of massive stone retaining walls and foundations which unite house and site.[16]

An anonymous article of August 1912, possibly by Stickley, stressed the sincerity of Greene and Greene houses as shown in "low, widespreading roof lines, the solid yet picturesque walls, the frank use of structural beams, the luxurious spaces of porch and balcony and the quiet loveliness of the interior."[17] Henry Greene remarked on the Robert Pitcairn, Jr., house (plate 105), built in 1906:

> The whole construction was carefully thought out and there was a reason for every detail. The idea was to eliminate everything unnecessary, to make the whole as direct and simple as possible, but always with the beautiful in mind as the final goal.[18]

104. Theodore Irwin house, Charles and Henry Greene, Pasadena, California, 1906, exterior detail. *The Craftsman* 12, no. 4 (July 1907): following 446.

The author saw the simplicity of their work as "the thing that is going to make California's architecture a vital record in the chronicle of the nation and help push forward the art of home-building toward our great democratic ideal."[19] Greene and Greene buildings, however, had an expensive simplicity because

105. Robert Pitcairn, Jr., house, Charles and Henry Greene, Pasadena, California, 1906, exterior detail. *The Craftsman* 22, no. 5 (August 1912): following 536.

of the hand labor necessary to shape the wood. They would have been beyond the reach of the middle-class pocketbook.

Stickley's admiration for Irving Gill (1870–1936), another California architect, is reflected in the several *Craftsman* articles on his work. Ellen

106. Henry H. Timkins house, Irving Gill, San Diego, California, exterior. *The Craftsman* 24, no. 4 (July 1913): 435.

Roorbach's perceptive 1913 article on Gill's Henry H. Timkins house (plate 106) in San Diego outlines the main characteristics of his mature work:

> There are several points about the construction of this particular house that deserve especial attention. In the first place its deliberate simplicity cannot be overlooked. It compels attention. It calls to mind Schiller's observation that 'The artist may be known rather by what he omits.' The architect Irving J. Gill, with pioneer courage resolved to go back to certain fixed principles like the line, square and cube, and to build from them with as little deviation as possible, omitting everything useless from a structural point of view. He saw that ornament was a non-essential.[20]

Irving Gill wrote about his own intentions in architecture in a 1916 *Craftsman* article, all but quoting Roorbach:

> Any deviation from simplicity results in a loss of dignity. Ornaments tend to cheapen rather than enrich, they acknowledge inefficiency and weakness. A house cluttered up by complex ornament means that the designer was aware that his work lacked purity of line and

perfection of proportion, so he endeavored to cover its imperfection by adding on detail, hoping thus to distract the attention of the observer from the fundamental weakness of his design. If we omit everything useless from the structural point of view we will come to see the great beauty of straight lines, to see the charm that lies in perspective, the force of light and shade, the power in balanced masses, the fascination of color that plays upon a smooth wall left free to report the passing of a cloud or nearness of a flower, the furious rush of storm and the burning stillness of summer suns.[21]

Here again, we see those key words of the Craftsman Movement, "simplicity" and "structural" which were applied to Greene and Greene houses. Gill's "simplicity" was quite different from that of the Greenes. Gill's material was concrete or hollow tiles as opposed to wood. The commonality of these contemporaries rests in their respect for craftsmanship and in their elimination of extraneous details. As William H. Jordy has pointed out, Gill and the Greenes also had in common the horizontality of their houses, the projection of interior space into the garden, the regionalism of their California setting, and the relationship of their designs to architecture of the past.[22]

Gill's Timkins house, a typical example of his mature work, is of interest for seemingly contradictory reasons. Its material and form are innovative, akin to progressive European architecture of the period. Gill used flush interior moldings and doors without panels. Magnesite, a very smooth material, was used for kitchen counters with rounded edges; floor coverings and wainscoting for the porches and bathrooms were also made of magnesite, and the bathtub was boxed with this material for ease of cleaning.[23] On the other hand, the U floor plan around a courtyard on a walled site and the exterior with its arched openings, balcony, and flat roof recalls the Spanish missions of California's past. Gill's distillation of historic architectural form to create the new is remarkable.

Stickley probably saw houses designed by Gill and the Greenes during his visits to California. He may even have met the architects. The "simplicity" and "honesty" of California houses appealed to him, and he always emphasized these qualities in his own designs and writings. He must have considered California houses "democratic" although the large homes by Gill and the Greenes were too expensive for the average family.

Even though there was a recurrent emphasis on "American" and "democratic" architecture in *The Craftsman,* Stickley remained interested in English architects. Barry Parker (1867–1947), an English architect, wrote a twenty-eight-article series on English country houses for *The Craftsman* between 1910 and 1912. Parker and his partner, Raymond Unwin (1863–1940), were important for their involvement in the Garden City Movement as well as their architecture and numerous publications. Their book, *The Art of Building a Home* (1901), had been reviewed by Irene Sargent for *The Craftsman* in 1902. It is easy to understand why Stickley published the Parker series; their design philosophies were similar, and Parker's houses, in many respects similar to designs by Baillie Scott and Voysey, appealed to Stickley.

Parker's articles, based in part on *The Art of Building a Home,* were practical examinations of the various considerations in planning a house. For example, "Modern Country Homes in England: Number Three" begins with a discussion of the placement of doors, windows, and fireplace so that drafts might be avoided and natural light utilized. Parker and Unwin's C. F. Goodfellow house, built in 1903–1904 in Northwood near Stoke-on-Trent, England, is used as an example of the proper relationship of a fireplace to the inglenook seats flanking it (plate 107). Since full floor plans, twelve exterior and interior photographs, and a section drawing are included in the article, it is obvious that the house as a whole was considered important.[24] The Goodfellow house exemplifies the qualities of "light, air and cheerfulness" considered by Parker and Unwin to be paramount for mental health and family happiness.[25] These qualities were also important to Stickley who had no obstructing curtains in his own house. The furniture in the Goodfellow house would have pleased Stickley since it too was structural and simple in design.

In a wider sense Stickley was interested in Parker and Unwin because of their contributions to "civic improvement," which meant planned communities to Stickley. Although *The Craftsman* published occasional articles on urban design, the concept of the planned village or suburb was more to Stickley's liking. The ideal of the healthful and simple way of life in a rural or village setting was a part of the English Arts and Crafts Movement dating back to William Morris or even further back to John Ruskin. The working conditions and environment of average workers had concerned both Ruskin and Morris who had seen the medieval period as an ideal time when workers had a vital role in a real community rather than being crowded together in the industrialized, anonymous city.

142   The early English factory town of Bournville, established in 1895 by

107. C. F. Goodfellow house, Barry Parker and Raymond Unwin, Northwood near Stoke-on-Trent, England, 1903–1904, inglenook. *The Craftsman* 18, no. 3 (June 1910): 328.

George Cadbury for his chocolate factory workers, was described in glowing detail in *The Craftsman*. Here each house, semidetached or built in a four-unit block, had its own garden already begun before the tenant moved in. For his workers Cadbury provided such amenities as recreation fields, a public school, a village hall, and the appropriately named Ruskin Hall used for lectures and classes.[26]

Raymond Unwin contributed an article on improvements to existing towns to *The Craftsman* while he and Barry Parker were planning Letchworth, the first garden city (1903–1905) and Hampstead Garden Suburb (1905 and later) near London. He pleaded for "Civic Art" which would include carefully planned streets oriented toward views and sometimes flanked by rows of trees, parks, gardens, and houses built in connected units to allow for united open spaces. He feared that such amenities would be difficult to achieve in existing towns but suggested the establishment of zoning laws and planning boards to control town development for the community interest as opposed to haphazard development by individual property owners.[27]

In 1909, Stickley wrote an article on the growth of the Garden City Movement which seems to have been inspired by his personal inspection of Letchworth and Hampstead Garden Suburb. He began his article with a definition of the ideal city:

> a community which will unite with the fullest civic life and opportunity, the freedom and healthfulness of the country, and in which the citizens, merely because of their citizenship, will be entitled to share in all the benefits of the commonwealth. In this ideal community, as it has been outlined for us over and over again, the very failings of human nature, — the self-seeking and combativeness which are the life blood of individualism, — will be transmuted by the new conditions of life into recognition of, and striving for, the wider good which includes the whole community; class antagonism will be replaced by mutual understanding and good will, and all alike will have the opportunity to live, work and enjoy.[28]

Here again, he looked to mutual cooperation as the best way to a happy life for all people. He thought that control of the garden city by a cooperative of tenants was vital to the success of such an enterprise.

The idea of participatory cooperation did not extend to a classless society. In a discussion of Hampstead Garden Suburb, Stickley approved the division of the community into one-to-three-acre sites for large houses in one area and worker houses in another; he thought that "friendly mingling of all classes" would result from the overall plan which he compared to an English village on a large scale. He endorsed the attention of Parker and Unwin to preservation of natural landscape features and their plan to limit housing to no more than twelve units per acre so that private gardens and public greens might be provided for all. He admired the architecture in general and singled out a quadrangle of sixty apartments by Baillie Scott and another apartment house with common kitchens and laundry for special praise.

Stickley became almost poetic toward the end of his article and concluded it with a pledge of *Craftsman* support:

> When it is remembered that a large part of the dwellers in this suburb are working people from the heart of London, whose means would allow them only one or two tenement rooms in the most crowded districts of the city, it is possible to realize what such a suburb means. Walking through the streets at twilight it is a distinct comfort to anyone interested in social betterment to pass a group of cottages and see the men, who have come home from their day's work, sociably engaged in weeding or hoeing and calling bits of chaff or gossip to one another across the low hedges which divide their gardens, while the women sit with their sewing in the doorways and the children play on the green that is common to all. This is no fancy picture; it may be seen anywhere at any time when the weather is warm enough in Hampstead Garden Suburb, and the best of it is that it may also be seen in the similar villages which are growing up in a dozen different places throughout England. We who are interested in civic improvement in America would do well to add to our plans for magnificent parkways, costly boulevards and great city extensions some consideration of the significance of this garden village movement and what it would mean if it were introduced and put on an effective working basis in this country. With all our energy, England has shot far ahead of us in this matter and from this time forward *The Craftsman* means to do all within its power to keep its readers alive to what might be done here if we could only manage to set aside the real estate speculator and all his fellows, and try the experiment of developing some of the open land near our own great cities along the lines pursued so successfully by the promoters of the English garden village.[29]

True to his pledge, *The Craftsman* did continue in its support of the Garden City Movement. The American Garden City Suburb of Forest Hills Gardens (plate 108) on Long Island, New York, was described and pictured in a 1911 *Craftsman* article. Then in its planning stage, Forest Hills was sponsored by the Russell Sage Foundation as a model project. The overall site plan was done by Frederick Law Olmsted, Jr., and Grosvenor Atterbury, an architect admired by Stickley, was architectural consultant and designer of many of its English-Arts-and-Crafts-inspired buildings. Like Hampstead Garden Suburb,

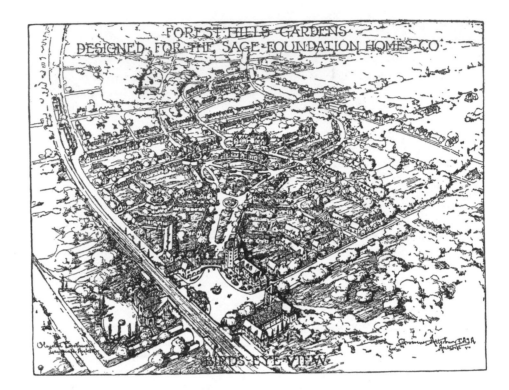

108. Forest Hills Gardens, Grosvenor Atterbury and Frederick Law Olmsted, Jr., Long Island, New York, 1909–1912, birdseye view. *The Craftsman* 19, no. 5 (February 1911): 448.

Forest Hills was to have mixed housing ranging from small apartments in its commercial area to single houses on large sites. The master plan provided for ten classifications of buildings. The *Craftsman* article warned readers that Forest Hills would be too expensive for low-paid workers, apparently in response to an earlier announcement that it was to be a "working men's colony." Although houses could be rented, tenants were encouraged to build their own homes, subject to design guidelines.[31] Much of the original scheme for Forest Hills with its provisions for residential and commercial structures was accomplished.[30]

The Craftsman carried articles on "civic improvements" in Boston and its suburbs and pointed out the merits of planning in such diverse towns as Great Falls, Montana, and Santa Barbara, California.[31] Stickley's interest in town planning was an extension of his concern for mutual cooperation and his preoccupation with the single-family house. While the planners of garden cities saw the economic necessity for grouped housing to provide room for green spaces and Stickley could see the advantages of this concept, he had that typical American love for the house on its own plot of land. Thus his philosophy contained elements of mutuality and individuality which might be considered contradictory.

The Craftsman contributed to public awareness of many issues which interested Stickley. He had the insight to choose many of the country's leading architects as subjects of articles and even commissioned them to write about their design philosophies. Even though he largely ignored the Prairie school, he published articles by Louis Sullivan and Purcell and Elmslie on functionalism. He chose the work of the Greene brothers and Gill as examples of the best houses in California to illustrate his concepts of honesty and simplicity in architecture. Through Barry Parker's *Craftsman* articles he presented practical advice and good examples of English Arts and Crafts architecture to his readers. He obviously hoped to inspire readers through the articles on garden cities. His concern for good design is reflected in the range of *Craftsman* articles on architecture and planning. These were the same concerns which had led Stickley to design his Craftsman houses.

8

THE COLLAPSE OF
THE CRAFTSMAN EMPIRE

USTAV STICKLEY was rarely content with the status quo; during all the years of his involvement with the Arts and Crafts Movement, he continued to widen his Craftsman horizons. This restless expansion was both his glory and a major cause of his downfall. Beginning with the development of a successful furniture business, he added *The Craftsman* to his activities and soon became involved with architecture, first as Craftsman homes in his magazine, later and briefly as a Craftsman house builder, and finally as a custom designer of houses. During this period, his Craftsman furniture became more widely available to the public. By January 1914, there were fifty furniture dealers throughout the country who sold Craftsman products along with their other lines. In addition there were Craftsman stores in Boston at 468 Boylston Street, and in Washington at 1512 H Street N.W.[1]

In keeping with his ever-widening involvements, he had established furniture showrooms and a publishing office in New York City at 29 West Thirty-fourth Street, after his Syracuse "Craftsman Building," the Crouse Stables, was sold in 1905. These new headquarters were soon outgrown, and the publishing office was moved to 41 West Thirty-fourth Street in 1908. Thus New York was the real headquarters of Stickley's activities beginning in 1905, although his factory remained in Eastwood, New York.

During the period in which his Craftsman furniture was most popular, Gustav Stickley had to contend with many competitors who emulated his designs and sometimes sold their similar furniture at lower prices. Among his competitors were his own brothers, Charles and Albert Stickley who had established their Stickley Brothers Company in Grand Rapids, Michigan, in 1891 and made furniture labeled "Quaint" or "Arts and Crafts" which resembled Gustav's Craftsman designs.[2] Albert remained in Grand Rapids, but Charles Stickley returned to Binghamton, New York, where he had earlier worked in the family furniture business with Gustav and Albert. There, Charles

Stickley became the manager of the Stickley and Brandt Chair Company which made its own versions of mission furniture.

Leopold Stickley (1869–1957), always called Lee by family and friends, had been Gustav's foreman when he started his Eastwood factory, and even earlier they had worked together in the family businesses in Binghamton and nearby Brandt, Pennsylvania.[3] In 1902, Leopold and another brother, J. George Stickley, started a furniture factory in Fayetteville, New York, a village near Syracuse.[4] Their new business was called the Onondaga Shops after the county in which it was located. George Stickley was the firm's salesman while Lee managed the factory; Lee also supplied the basic designs for the furniture which was detailed by Donald Hanson. After a slow start, Lee and George began to expand, and in 1905 they issued their first catalog. By 1910, they were calling their furniture "Handcraft," obviously inspired by Gustav Stickley's Craftsman label. For a time, Lee and George even used a handscrew marking device[5] in imitation of Gustav's medieval compass device. Not only did the "Handcraft" label and handscrew imitate Gustav's labels, but more importantly, the L. and J. G. Stickley designs emulated those of their eldest brother, a situation which must have infuriated Gustav.

Like most Craftsman furniture, L. and J. G. Stickley mission furniture was made of fumed oak and usually had straight lines. Two pieces illustrated in the c. 1914 L. and J. G. Stickley catalog are good examples of their method of combining Craftsman details to create pieces which are not Craftsman copies but nevertheless indebted to Craftsman furniture for inspiration. One of their straight chairs (plate 109) has a curved seat support similar to that used by Harvey Ellis in Craftsman designs so many years earlier (plate 34) and the vertical back slats used for various Craftsman chairs. The height of the L. and J. G. Stickley chair is somewhat lower than the Ellis chair and the general proportions are closer to most of Gustav Stickley's later chairs (plate 37). An L. and J. G. Stickley bookcase (plate 110) has the general proportions of a Craftsman piece (plate 40) and even the same kind of curved top; the tenon and key joints of the Fayetteville bookcase, however, are like those used in an even earlier Craftsman piece (plate 39) L. and J. G. Stickley manufactured a large line of furniture like their eldest brother, often emulating him but sometimes producing an excellent piece for which there is no Craftsman counterpart. A settle also illustrated in their c. 1914 catalog (plate 111) is such a piece. It has spindle back and sides like earlier Craftsman chairs but curved side aprons rather than straight ones. It has an elegance of its own quite unlike any Craftsman settles which tended to be heavier in their proportions.

109. Side chair, L. and J. G. Stickley,
c. 1914. *The Work of L. and J. G.
Stickley, Fayetteville, New York,*
[c. 1914], p. 14.

110. Bookcase, L. and J. G. Stickley, c. 1914.
*The Work of L. and J. G. Stickley, Fayetteville,
New York,* [c. 1914], p. 38.

111. Settle, L. and J. G. Stickley, c. 1914. *The Work of L. and J. G. Stickley, Fayetteville, New
York,* [c. 1914], p. 27.

151

In their c. 1914 catalog, L. and J. G. Stickley proudly stated that their furniture was:

> a product that claims and fills the entire time of its producers, who indulge in no other occupation....Furniture building, it is believed, is in itself important work, demanding the entire time of the modern craftsmen who attempt it.[6]

This is an obvious allusion to Gustav Stickley's many activities with the implication that Gustav did not devote enough attention to his furniture making. Perhaps Lee and George were correct in their statement; in the long run they chose the better financial course since L. and J. G. Stickley Furniture Company is still a going concern in Fayetteville, and Gustav Stickley was forced into bankruptcy. L. and J. G. Stickley began to replace their Arts and Crafts furniture designs with cherry colonial reproductions in the early 1920s, seeing that their customers had lost interest in their earlier designs.

Gustav Stickley's final expansion took place in 1913. In May of that year, he proudly announced to his readers that a new Craftsman Building would open in New York in time for the tenth anniversary of *The Craftsman*.[7] This new headquarters at 6 East Thirty-ninth Street was located in the city's prime shopping district only a few steps east of Fifth Avenue. On one side it faced Bonwit Teller, while the ultrarespectable Union League Club was its neighbor across Thirty-ninth Street. Such fashionable stores as Lord and Taylor, Tiffany's, and Franklin Simon were nearby. The new Craftsman Building was an expensive piece of real estate; the first year's lease cost $50,000, and in subsequent years the lease was to cost $61,000.[8]

The Craftsman Building (plate 112) was twelve stories tall and two hundred feet deep; in it all the Craftsman enterprises except furniture manufacturing were housed under one roof. The lower four stories were used as showrooms for furniture, draperies, and rugs. As might be expected, Craftsman oak and wicker furniture and other products from the Craftsman workshops were prominently displayed. Apparently some "Colonial" furniture was shown as well. Floors five through eight housed the Craftsman Permanent Homebuilder's Exposition, a new Stickley enterprise in which various manufacturers rented space to exhibit garden supplies, home equipment, various building materials, and model rooms with special wall finishes. Stickley

THE CRAFTSMAN RESTAURANT

THE CRAFTSMAN CLUB-ROOMS
LIBRARY AND LECTURE HALL

THE CRAFTSMAN MAGAZINE
ARCHITECTURAL AND SERVICE DEPTS.

CRAFTSMAN WORKSHOPS

Building Materials

Home Decoration
Model Rooms

Home Equipment

Garden and Grounds

THE
CRAFTSMAN
PERMANENT
HOMEBUILDERS'
EXPOSITION

RUGS——INTERIOR DECORATING

DRAPERIES AND HOUSE FURNISHINGS

GENERAL FURNITURE DISPLAY

CRAFTSMAN FURNITURE DISPLAY

112. Craftsman Building, New York, 1913, exterior. *The Craftsman* 25, no. 4 (January 1914): 4a.

thought of his new building as a design center where customers could select every item necessary for building and furnishing a Craftsman home under one roof. Presumably, *Craftsman* advertisers were prime candidates to rent exhibition space.

The ninth floor housed the Craftsman Workshops where crafts were demonstrated to the public. Customers who had seen the building products at the permanent exhibit could proceed to the tenth floor to discuss house plans with the Craftsman Architects. The editorial offices of *The Craftsman* were also on the tenth floor. Stickley wanted customers to feel at home in his building; for their comfort he provided club rooms, a library, a lecture room, and rest rooms on the eleventh floor. Tired customers could relax here after shopping or meet friends in a Craftsman atmosphere.

Since his building was to be homelike, Stickley installed a restaurant on the top floor (plate 113). Customers could dine on wholesome meat and eggs sent into the city from Craftsman Farms in a Craftsman ambience complete with Grueby tiled fireplace, Craftsman furniture, and specially designed china, silver, and glassware marked with the Craftsman compass symbol.[9] A visit to the Craftsman Building must have been a gratifying experience for customers who were devotees of the Arts and Crafts Movement. There all the goods so often featured in *The Craftsman* were on display. Stickley must have viewed his headquarters as the fulfillment of his dreams of the total Craftsman environment.

While the Craftsman Building was being discussed in *The Craftsman* and drawing its first customers, ominous rumblings of financial problems were becoming apparent behind the scenes. Ben Wiles, Stickley's son-in-law and business manager, warned that the Craftsman Building was too expensive for Stickley's resources. His warning went unheeded as the building opened and Wiles resigned, moving back to Syracuse with his family.[10] Wiles was correct in his assessment of Stickley's financial situation. The year 1913 marked the beginning of Stickley's gradual descent into bankruptcy. A letter of January 1913 reported that the Boston Craftsman store had lost more than $4,000 during 1912, but probably had enough stock on hand to balance the loss;[11] at the time this letter was written, Stickley was planning the New York Craftsman Building, and the Craftsman store in Washington was still solvent. *The Craftsman* retained its editorial vigor in 1913, but its gross income was only $86,806.02.[12] Meanwhile, the Craftsman architects were designing custom houses for a number of clients. It is tempting to imagine Mr. and Mrs. Evans, for example,

113. Craftsman Building, New York, 1913, restaurant. *The Craftsman* 25, no. 4 (January 1914): following 362.

visiting the new Craftsman Building to discuss the design of their Douglaston, Long Island, house[13] and to select Craftsman furnishings for it.

During the early 1910s, Gustav Stickley did not introduce many new Craftsman furniture designs. In his 1912 catalog he stated with confidence that "Most of my furniture was so carefully designed and well-proportioned in the first place, that even I with my advanced experience cannot improve upon it."[14] Perhaps because he felt that he could not improve on his furniture designs, he now began to experiment with colored finishes. The June 1915 *Craftsman* contained an article on the use of bright colors in the home;[15] along with illustrations of painted European peasant furniture, painted Craftsman armchairs were featured (plate 114). Two severely rectangular Craftsman

155

114. Armchairs, Gustav Stickley, 1915. *The Craftsman* 28, no. 3 (June 1915): following 246.

armchairs were glazed in black with painted lines to emphasize structure and small designs in red, blue, and green. Although some of Harvey Ellis' much earlier Craftsman furniture had been ornamented with inlaid designs of various woods and metals, no other Stickley pieces had been decorated with nonstructural motifs. Thus these painted chairs, probably experimental, represent a real departure from Stickley's design philosophy. While the painted lines emphasize form, the floral motifs are pure decoration, an element formerly shunned by Stickley.

More radical changes in Craftsman furniture designs followed as Stickley attempted to appeal to changing tastes. He denied that his new furniture designs were based on a historical period.[16] However, the new designs with their twined spindle legs (plate 115) seem to suggest American colonial and other historical models. The chairs retain the boxy outlines of earlier

Craftsman designs but have a new lightness since the wood components are rounded and more slender. The octagonal library table with its shaped lip, scalloped undershelf and paired spindle legs is a surprising design when compared with an earlier Craftsman table (plate 116). Stickley treated the new spindle designs with his colored finishes to produce a new line of furniture which he called Chromewald. Available in several colors, Chromewald furniture was Stickley's response to a new public interest in painted furniture as popularized by Elsie De Wolfe in her book, *The House in Good Taste* (1913), which advocated design concepts opposed to those which had formed the basis of Stickley's Craftsman designs.

The Craftsman magazine, always a good indicator of Stickley's interests, reflects the problems of the period following the hopeful grand opening of the expensive New York Craftsman Building. The vitality and innovative spirit of its early years are missing, and its articles often seemed rather commonplace. In 1915, only a few house designs were published and those which did appear were not as interesting as earlier cottages. In 1916, *The Craftsman* announced its intention of republishing the more than two hundred house plans on file. Unlike earlier plans which had been free, these reissued plans would be sold to readers.[17] In spite of a certain lack of new ideas after 1913, some issues of *The Craftsman* did have their bright spots, among them poetry and an article on the "New Poetry" by Amy Lowell in July 1916. Although Gustav Stickley remained in his position as editor of *The Craftsman* during most of these years, Mary Fanton Roberts (1871–1956) was managing editor and presumably she rather than Stickley ran the periodical.

It seems likely that the opening of the new Craftsman Building in 1913 as well as the later introduction of Chromewald furniture were attempts to recoup falling revenues. Unfortunately the expenses of running the twelve-story Craftsman headquarters only hastened the demise of the Craftsman enterprises, and the Chromewald furniture was not commercially successful. Gustav Stickley's business papers for the years 1913–16 record a gradual decrease in profits, attempts to consolidate debts, and a shrinkage of assets. Gustav Stickley's salary which had been $5,000 a year plus 10 percent of annual gross sales in 1912 was reduced to a flat $10,000 a year with no percentage of sales in 1914,[18] certainly a dramatic drop in personal income. On March 23, 1915, a petition of bankruptcy was filed by Gustav Stickley, The Craftsman, Inc.[19] On May 20, 1915, a letter sent to all those owed money by the corporation stated that total liabilities amounted to $229,705.64.[20]

Although *The Craftsman* continued publication through December 1916, the corporation was essentially dead more than a year earlier. Stickley lost his magazine, his furniture factory, the Craftsman Building, and Craftsman Farms. There were a number of reasons for the failure of his business ventures, among them the overzealous expansion into the Craftsman Building and a change in taste on the part of the public which no longer admired the structural purity of the Craftsman furniture which had made Stickley famous. Perhaps the primary reason for Stickley's financial failure was his tendency to take on ever more projects until he reached the point where he simply could not manage all his interests. One of the saddest results of the bankruptcy was reported in a letter discussing the use of the Craftsman name by others, a practice which had infuriated Stickley on earlier occasions. Now Stickley no longer cared to bother about it.[21] The Craftsman name, and perhaps the philosophy behind that name, so important to Gustav Stickley for so long, no longer mattered very much.

The physical assets of the Craftsman corporations were disposed of in various ways. *The Craftsman* merged with *Art World* in January 1917. In May 1917, Mary Fanton Roberts, former managing editor of *The Craftsman* initiated *The Touchstone,* a magazine much like *The Craftsman* in format, with most of *The Craftsman* staff. Although the first issue of *The Touchstone* contained a short note of congratulations from Stickley, he was never mentioned editorially within its pages.

The period immediately after the Craftsman bankruptcy was a restless time for Stickley. In 1917, he went to Kenosha, Wisconsin, to work for the Simmons Company as a consultant. Although he earned a large salary, he remained only a short time.[22] He then returned to Syracuse, joining his brothers briefly in 1917–18 in a furniture manufacturing concern called Stickley Associated Cabinetmakers. In this short lived collaboration, J. George and Leopold Stickley of Fayetteville, New York, were also joined by Albert Stickley of Grand Rapids, Michigan. Gustav Stickley apparently had difficulty in working with his brothers, and soon their association fell apart. The Fayetteville brothers, J. George and Leopold, continued to operate the former Craftsman factory in Eastwood.[23]

In 1918, Gustav Stickley was sixty years old, still of an age to accomplish a great deal had he wanted further glories. His wife died in 1918, but he was to live for twenty-four years. He soon moved back into the Syracuse house he had built so many years earlier. There he had developed the Craftsman

115. Armchairs and table, Gustav
Stickley, 1916. *The Craftsman* 29, no. 5
(February 1916): following 532.

116. Table, Gustav Stickley, 1904.
*Cabinet Work from the Craftsman
Workshops,* c. 1904, in Stephen Gray and
Robert Edwards, eds., *Collected Works
of Gustav Stickley* (New York: Turn of
the Century Editions, 1981), p. 82.

interior detailing which had contributed so much to his reputation. Now his son-in-law, Ben Wiles, his daughter, Barbara Wiles, and his grandchildren lived there. Gustav Stickley lived on the third floor where an apartment was created for him. In the small kitchen of his apartment, he experimented with the furniture finishes which fascinated him. Barbara Wiles later recalled the smell of varnish cooking on the stove and the frequent visits of the plumber who had to remove varnish residues from clogged pipes.[24]

Stickley occasionally visited the furniture craftsmen who had earlier worked for him and were later employed by his brothers, J. George and Leopold. These workmen were always glad to see him. When he died after a brief illness on April 21, 1942, these workmen appeared as a group at his funeral to offer a last tribute.[25] He left no will because there was no estate to be divided among his heirs.

It seems strange that Gustav Stickley who had been so active from the 1890s to 1916, should have done so little in the long years following his bankruptcy. Perhaps his spirit was broken when his financial collapse took away everything he had built. He had been totally involved in his many Craftsman activities, and he was a guiding light of the Arts and Crafts Movement in the United States. He must have felt that everything he stood for had been rejected by the public with whom he felt a close bond. Remarkably, he never expressed any bitterness at the failure of his business ventures.[26] He survived with dignity although he was a forgotten man when he died.

Gustav Stickley's Craftsman furniture has been rediscovered in recent years. Several Craftsman furniture catalogs have been republished in whole or in part. Selected articles from *The Craftsman* and some Craftsman house designs have been republished.[27] The fortunate families who now live in Craftsman homes are enthusiastic about the quality of life within their walls. Each of Stickley's accomplishments — Craftsman furniture, *The Craftsman,* Craftsman homes — is closely connected with the other two since the three creative areas were integral parts of his Craftsman Movement.

Stickley is the best person to explain what his Craftsman Movement meant. When his New York Craftsman Building had just opened in 1913, he wrote an article on the origin and development of the movement, comparing it to the organic growth of a tree which must keep growing:

A movement that has grown as this one has, must keep on growing. People need it; they wouldn't let me stop even if I wanted to.

As I think the matter over, it comes to me more and more clearly that here lies the true explanation — that it is a *movement,* and not merely an individual enterprise. It must either grow or decay; it cannot stand still. For a movement is like a tree—if it once gets a firm hold in the soil, if it has its *roots in the ground,* it cannot help growing. Barring accidents, nothing can stop it....

Fifteen years ago this Movement started. It had its origin in a few simple chairs. Yet such sound principles of craftsmanship inspired their conception, and such popular response did their making invoke, that out of this seemingly insignificant beginning developed all that the word "Craftsman" now implies.

Today the Craftsman Movement stands not only for simple, well made furniture, conceived in the spirit of true craftsmanship, designed for beauty as well as comfort, and built to last, it stands also for a distinct type of American architecture, for well built, democratic homes, planned for and owned by the people who live in them, homes that solve the servant problem by their simple, pleasant arrangement, and meet the needs of wholesome family life. Big, light, airy living rooms that foster the social spirit are a part of its purpose; it holds as essential the open fireplace as the natural nucleus for happy indoor life. The plain yet decorative woodwork and built-in fittings that help to simplify housework and produce a restful, homelike atmosphere are inherent in its plan. The sheltered places for outdoor dining, rest and play, and the healthful sleeping porch which is coming to be recognized as so vital a part of the modern home are inevitably a part of the Craftsman home. It stands, too, for the companionship of gardens, the wholesomeness of country and suburban living and the health and efficiency which these imply. It aims to be instrumental in the restoration of the people to the land and the land to the people. It is always for progress, for scientific farming, for closer coöperation between producer and consumer, and less waste in both agricultural and industrial fields. It stands for the rights of the children to health and happiness, through an education that will develop hands as well as heads; an education that will give them that love and enthusiasm for useful work which is every child's rightful heritage, and fit them to take their places as efficient members of a great democracy. Civic improvement is close to its heart, political, as well as social and industrial progress; it desires to strengthen honest craftsmanship in every branch of human activity, and strives for a form of art which shall express the spirit of the American people....

161

At first the furniture I made was on the usual conventional lines; but as the years went by and I experimented with the various forms of construction and design, I began to understand better what good furniture and true craftsmanship meant. I tried to make pieces that would be first of all practical and comfortable, that would last a man's lifetime without being much the worse for wear; the kind of things one could take pride in handing down to one's grandchildren. I wanted them to be beautiful, too, not with the superficial prettiness of applied ornament, but with that inherent decorative quality which comes from good proportions, mellow finish and harmonious coloring. And to these ends I tried always to choose strong, serviceable materials, with the sort of texture, design and coloring that would result in a genuine, homelike charm.

I did not realize at the time that in making those few pieces of strong, simple furniture, I had started a new movement. Others saw it and prophesied a far-reaching development. To me it was only furniture; to them it was religion. And eventually it became religion with me as well.

Thus, unconsciously a Craftsman style was evolved and developed, a style that gradually found its way into the homes of the people, pushing out a branch here, a branch there, first in one direction and then in another, wherever it met with sympathy and encouragement.

The next thing that naturally suggested itself was the need of a broader medium of expression for these ideas of craftsmanship and home-making; the need of some definite, organized plan for reaching people who, I felt sure, would be interested in what I was trying to accomplish; some means of getting into direct communication with them, of entering, so to speak, into their very homes. And so, in October, nineteen hundred and one, the Craftsman Movement sent forth another branch, full of hope and promise—the first number of THE CRAFTSMAN Magazine. . . .

In the magazine I have striven from the beginning to present the work and opinions of others in sympathy with my ideas, as well as my own suggestions regarding home-making, and point of view about the problems of the day. In as direct, authentic and beautiful fashion as I could, I have set forth what seemed the best and most representative work of artists, craftsmen, architects and other workers in significant fields, both in this country and abroad; reviewing and illustrating whatever I believed would prove helpful to those men and women of America who needed stimulus to spur them on to finer achievement.

But a healthy movement, like a healthy tree, does not grow merely in one or two directions. And while the magazine was sending out its branches and spreading its influence over American homes wherever it could reach throughout the country, the main trunk of the movement was sending forth still other branches.

For all this time the original source of the movement, the furniture, had been developing and finding its way to home-loving people who wanted simple, serviceable things. And as the demand grew, I became more and more interested in every detail of the home environment, for I saw that the way a man's house was planned and built had as much influence upon his family's health and happiness as had the furniture they lived with. Besides, such unassuming furnishings as mine were out of place in elaborate over-ornamented interiors. They needed the sort of rooms and woodwork and exterior that would be in keeping with their own more homelike qualities. They suggested, by their sturdy build and friendly finish, an equally sturdy and friendly type of architecture. This being the case, why not build the kind of homes that would be in sympathy with the Craftsman ideal? Thus was evolved what has since come to be known as Craftsman architecture.

I planned these houses with a big living room because I believed in having a comfortable place for general family life, large enough to eliminate that sense of friction which is so apt to invade a cramped and narrow home. In this room I planned a generous fireplace, because I knew that people were longing to return to the oldtime comfort and hospitality that centered so pleasantly around the open hearth. And this fireplace became one of the most characteristic features of my plans — even developing later, after much scientific study and experiment, into a means of heating and ventilating the whole house.

The rest of the space in a Craftsman house I arranged compactly, with as few partitions as possible for the sake of economy and the simplifying of work. More often than not the rooms were all on one floor, to eliminate the trouble of stair-climbing, and special attention was paid to the kitchen and other parts where the maid or housewife would have to spend much time, and which consequently should be light, cheerful and convenient.

Then the question naturally suggested itself — why build

homes in the city? Why live in tall buildings, in rows and solid blocks, with a minimum of air and light and garden space, when there is so much beautiful country within reach? Why not live where there is plenty of fresh air and sunshine, plenty of room to grow flowers and vegetables, to rest and exercise out of doors? Why not get "back to the land?"

Thinking and working along these lines, the houses I planned naturally began to take on certain aspects of country and suburban living — big porches for outdoor work and rest and play, dining porches, sleeping balconies, pergolas and other garden features that would link the interior closely with the outdoor life.

The next thing that suggested itself was that people, instead of living in houses built merely for speculation, should plan and build and *own* their own homes — even the people who could afford only a little four or five-room cottage or bungalow. And it seemed to me that if these homes were to be *theirs* in the fullest sense of the word, they must give their own time, thought and energy to the planning of each detail, and then make sure that the architect and builder carried out their ideas in an economical, practical and beautiful way.

These opinions I naturally expressed in THE CRAFTSMAN Magazine, where each month I published one or more of my house designs, thus making them available to readers in every part of the world. I published floor plans and perspective views of both interior and exterior, with practical advice as to construction, finish, furnishing and decorating schemes. People began to look more and more to this magazine as a source of encouragement and aid. Men and women who were expecting to build and furnish their own homes would write to me for plans, ask my advice about different methods of construction or different kinds of wood finishes, or want me to make suggestions for interior decorations and color schemes. And out of these inquiries and their answers, Craftsman Service developed — another branch of the constantly growing Craftsman Movement.

As I was continually advising people to build their own homes in a simple, practical fashion, the next thing that inevitably suggested itself was that I should *actually help them to do it;* show them the various building materials, point out the qualities and uses of each, explain the different methods of construction, teach them how to choose the most serviceable and appropriate things, how to plan wisely and build well.

So I began to bring together for their inspection samples of building materials, paints and finishes, miniature models of cottages and bungalows, and household devices of various kinds. But I soon found that three floors occupied by my architectural, editorial and circulation forces were quite inadequate to allow a suitable display or to accommodate with comfort all my visitors. It became necessary to move into more spacious and convenient quarters; hence the Craftsman Movement has branched out into the new Craftsman Building....

Thus, like the tree, out of what seemed a small and insignificant beginning, has the Craftsman Movement grown. Not because I consciously willed or planned it; not because of great capital or prestige; but simply because it had its *roots in the ground.* It grew out of actual spiritual needs and physical conditions. It drew life from the warm, fertile soil of the people's interest and enthusiasm. And it depends upon their continued love and help, as well as upon my own endeavor, to keep its branches green, to make it grow into still farther-reaching strength and still wider efficiency.[28]

Gustav Stickley's Craftsman furniture, solid, sturdy, "primitive," and "structural," might be considered among the earliest modern designs in the United States. He eliminated the machine-made ornamentation of late-nineteenth-century American furniture and created furniture which depended on honest expression of structure for its characteristic design qualities. For a short time Harvey Ellis contributed elements of grace and elegance of proportion to Stickley's heavier designs. If imitation is a form of flattery, he should have felt very flattered. His brothers—Leopold, J. George, Charles, and Albert — were often his closest followers although the brothers in Fayetteville developed some fine designs of their own. Soon even Sears Roebuck was selling inexpensive mission oak furniture which resembled Gustav Stickley's more expensive and better quality Craftsman pieces.

Stickley was not alone in designing innovative furniture in the early years of the twentieth century; other designers, also inspired by William Morris and other leaders of the English Arts and Crafts Movement, were producing similar furniture. Frank Lloyd Wright, George Grant Elmslie, George Maher, and the Greene brothers, all architects, were designing furniture with details and proportions akin to Craftsman furniture between 1900 and 1916. These architects designed furniture to be used in houses they designed while Stickley designed houses to fit his furniture. There were interesting links between Stickley and most of these architects. He publicized the work of the Greene brothers beginning in 1907, and they chose one of his screens for their Gamble house (1907–1909) in Pasadena, California. Elmslie recommended Stickley chairs and tables for the Henry B. Babson house (1907) in Riverside, Illinois.[29] George Maher adapted a Craftsman plan for the Raymond Riordon house in Rolling Prairie, Indiana.[30] Stickley furniture was sometimes used in Frank Lloyd Wright-designed houses, but probably Wright preferred to design his own furniture whenever possible. Although Stickley was hardly alone in designing Arts and Crafts furniture in the United States, he was a design leader in this furniture style and in many ways an innovator whose contribution to American design in this area alone is of great importance. Moreover, he made it possible for middle-class American families to have honestly designed, well-made Arts and Crafts furniture through his skills in merchandizing.

Stickley's Craftsman houses are a second contribution to American life style. Even though he was untrained in architecture, he contributed to the evolution of a house type, the bungalow, which represented the good life to many middle-class Americans. His house plans, available free to *Craftsman* readers, could be used anywhere in the country to build comfortable small homes which were not lavishly expensive. These houses were not meant for costly display; rather, they were meant to be centers of wholesome family life. They had the same structural honesty and simplicity of his furniture as was appropriate since Craftsman houses were meant to be perfect settings for his furniture. It seems likely that Stickley's Craftsman houses will never be totally documented because he urged potential home builders to modify plans to fit their own needs. Thus it is impossible to even estimate the number of Craftsman-inspired homes located in all parts of the United States.

Gustav Stickley was not alone in promoting the bungalow. Many bungalow books were published, among them William P. Comstock's *Bungalows, Camps and Mountain Homes* (c. 1915), Henry H. Saylor's *Bungalows, Their Design, Construction and Furnishings* (1911) and Frederick T. Hodgson's *Practical Bungalows and Cottages for Town and Country* (c. 1912).[31] Stickley republished plans of Craftsman bungalows, cottages, and larger houses in *Craftsman Homes* (c. 1909), *More Craftsman Homes* (1912), and *Craftsman Houses: A Book for Home Makers* (1913). These house books, by others as well as Stickley, included larger houses as well as small cottages.

There were two kinds of bungalow books: those which described the houses and their construction, that is, Saylor and Comstock, and those which pictured plans for sale, that is, Hodgson. *The Craftsman,* in addition to offering free plans to subscribers, contained advertisements for bungalow plan books published by others. Certainly Stickley contributed to the bungalow craze in the United States. Although he did not invent the American bungalow, his designs for small Craftsman houses had a distinctive form with a clarity of unornamented structure not usually found in other small houses of the period.

The clarity and simplicity of Stickley's bungalows and cottages carry through to larger Craftsman houses, especially those built by his own company. Because Stickley was able to control the quality of materials and construction of these houses, they are among his best works. However, since they were private commissions and usually not published in *The Craftsman,* they were not as influential in spreading the Craftsman house idea as his smaller houses.

In terms of influence on middle-class American housing, Stickley might even be considered as important as such masters as his contemporaries Frank Lloyd Wright and the Greene brothers. While Wright and the Greenes were trained architects designing custom houses for often well-to-do clients, Stickley, along with bungalow book publishers, was establishing a democratic, nonelitist architecture which was immediately appreciated by ordinary people. The importance of Craftsman architecture lies in its acceptance by the American middle class which built bungalows all over the country beginning in the early 1900s and continuing even into the 1930s.

The Craftsman began as Gustav Stickley's means of publicizing his furniture and the Arts and Crafts philosophy behind it. Soon *The Craftsman* became much more than an attractive little journal of design philosophy and furniture. Between 1901 and 1916, subscribers could gather information from its pages about a wide variety of subjects such as revolutionary social trends, recent American and European art and design, ethnic cultures and arts, construction and gardening methods, and, of course, Craftsman furniture and houses along with articles on architects and their designs. *The Craftsman* was both visionary and practical, presenting the philosophy of the Arts and Crafts Movement with its applications in everyday life. *The Craftsman* is still a pleasure to read; it is one of the best sources for material on the American Arts and Crafts Movement, and some of Stickley's articles are pertinent even now. Seldom has the leader of a movement had such an excellent opportunity to write about his beliefs and to publish his writings over a fifteen-year period.

Because Stickley was the controlling force behind *The Craftsman,* it reflects his interests and design philosophy so vividly that we almost feel we know the man.

A number of periodicals such as the English *Studio,* the American *International Studio,* and *The House Beautiful* influenced Stickley and probably competed with *The Craftsman* for readers interested in the Arts and Crafts Movement. Although *Ladies' Home Journal* contained innovative house designs by Wright and others in the early 1900s, it was primarily a woman's magazine. Another homemaker magazine, *House and Garden,* founded like *The Craftsman* in 1901, was elitist from the beginning and probably did not appeal to *Craftsman* readers. Even though competing magazines had some features in common with *The Craftsman,* only *The Craftsman* offered its readers Arts and Crafts philosophy plus free house plans, Craftsman furniture, and the stamp of one man's strong personality.

Gustav Stickley's integrated philosophy of life and art is reflected in his Craftsman furniture, houses, and magazine. That one man could do so much so well in such a coherent, common-sense way is remarkable. Stickley, both visionary and practical, selected his Craftsman label well; he was the essential craftsman. His motto, "Als ik kan," was well chosen to express his approach to life and art; he did as much as he could as well as he could.

NOTES

INTRODUCTION

1. For general information on the Arts and Crafts Movement, see Isabelle Anscombe and Charlotte Gere, *Arts and Crafts in Britain and America* (New York: Rizzoli, 1978); Robert Judson Clark, ed., *The Arts and Crafts Movement in America 1876–1916* (Princeton: Princeton University Press, 1972); Gillian Naylor, *The Arts and Crafts Movement* (Cambridge: MIT Press, 1971).

2. H. Allen Brooks, "Chicago Architecture: Its Debts to the Arts and Crafts," *Journal of the Society of Architectural Historians* 30, no. 4 (December 1971): 312–17; and Robert Winter, "American Sheaves from C.R.A. and Janet Ashbee," *Journal of the Society of Architectural Historians* 30, no.4 (December 1971): 317–22.

3. "Ledger, 1901–05," 76 x 101.11, "Business Papers of Gustav Stickley," Henry Francis Dupont Winterthur Museum, Winterthur, Delaware.

4. David M. Cathers, *Furniture of the American Arts and Crafts Movement: Stickley and Roycroft Mission Oak* (New York: New American Library, 1981), pp. 85–98.

5. Peg Weiss, ed., *Adelaide Alsop Robineau* (Syracuse: Syracuse University Press, 1981).

6. Cleota Reed Gabriel, "Irene Sargent: Rediscovering a Lost Legend," *Courier* 14 (Summer 1979): 4–9.

7. Cleota Reed Gabriel, *The Arts and Crafts Ideal: The Ward House, an Architect and his Craftsmen* (Syracuse: Institute for the Development of Evolutive Architecture, 1978).

1 –– GUSTAV STICKLEY'S EARLY YEARS

1. The major sources for details about the life of Gustav Stickley's early life are: *National Cyclopaedia of American Biography* (New York: James T. White, 1910), 14: 290–91; *Who's Who in America, 1906–07* (Chicago: A. N. Marquis, 1906), p. 172; John Crosby Freeman, "Forgotten Rebel: Gustav Stickley" (M.A. thesis, University of Delaware, 1964); John Crosby Freeman, *The Forgotten Rebel: Gustav Stickley and His Craftsman Mission Furniture* (Watkins Glen, N.Y.: Century House, 1966), pp. 8–14; and Kenneth L. DePrey, Sr., "Leopold Stickley Biography," 1957, Stickley Collection, Archives and Library, Edison Institute, Henry Ford Museum and Greenfield Village, Dearborn, Michigan. These sources do not agree on all points. For example, there may have been nine or eleven siblings in Gustav Stickley's family. Schuyler Brandt may or may not have been a Stickley relative. The chair factory in Brandt, Pennsylvania, where Stickley received his first training in furniture manufacturing, may have belonged to his uncle, Jacob Schlaeger, or to Schuyler Brandt. Dates given for Stickley's marriage are September 12, 1883, and September 5, 1887.

2. Gustav Stickley, *Chips from the Craftsman Workshops* (New York: Kalkhoff Co., 1906).

3. Ibid.

4. Ibid. In December 1891, the factory portion of the Stickley Brothers Company was incorporated with a capital of $30,000 as the Stickley and Brandt Chair Company. Schuyler C. Brandt was president and Charles Stickley was general manager; the firm went bankrupt in 1919. Charles Stickley and Schuyler C. Brandt took over the Stickley Brothers Company in 1890. See *Industries of Binghamton*

(Syracuse: H. J. Ornsbee, 1892) as published in Frederick W. Putnam, ed., *Documentary History of Broome County* (Binghamton: n.p., 1926), pp. 45, 118, 122; and William F. Seward, ed., *Binghamton and Broome County* (New York and Chicago: Lewis Historical Publishing Co., 1924), 2: 409.

5. The pertinent pages of *William's Binghamton City Directory* of 1888 are missing. Stickley and Simonds is listed in the 1889 and 1890 copies of the *Williams' Binghamton City Directory* (Binghamton: J. E. Williams, 1889 and 1890), pp. 395, 432, but not listed in 1891.

6. *Williams' Binghamton City Directory,* 1891, p. 12. See also Freeman, "Forgotten Rebel," p. 41 n. 37.

7. "Gustav Stickley Obituary," Syracuse *Post-Standard,* April 21, 1942, states that "During the administration of Governor Roswell P. Flower of New York State, he [Gustav Stickley] handled manufacturing operations in Auburn Prison, after which he came to Syracuse." Flower was New York governor, 1892–94.

8. Rita Reif, "The Master of Mission," *New York Times,* July 9, 1978, section 2, p. 27.

9. Freeman, *The Forgotten Rebel,* pp. 17–19, 52 n. 54 and n. 56. Apparently, the New York Legislature passed a law c. 1894 prohibiting the sale of convict-made products to the public; this exclusion of Stickley's main market was surely a reason for him to leave Auburn and start the Eastwood factory. Although the Stickley-Simonds Company factory was located in Eastwood, the company's stock certificates indicate Auburn as the location of incorporation.

10. *Boyd's Syracuse City Directory, 1893–94* (Syracuse: Boyd, 1893), p. 768.

The Yates, the grandest hotel in Syracuse, opened in 1892; its designer, Archimedes Russell, was one of the city's most prominent architects. The hotel was razed in 1971. See Evamaria Hardin, *Archimedes Russell, Upstate Architect* (Syracuse: Syracuse University Press, 1980), pp. 66–69; *Boyd's Syracuse City Directory, 1893–94,* p. 629.

11. *Boyd's Syracuse City Directory, 1896–97* and *1897–98,* p. 647.

12. For illustrations, see Freeman, "Forgotten Rebel," plates 23–27; and Freeman, *The Forgotten Rebel,* p. 15.

13. Syracuse *Post-Standard,* May 14, May 24, July 30, August 31, and September 16, 1899. Charles R. Flint, according to the *National Cyclopaedia of American Biography* 37, pp. 200–201, was involved in so many trusts that he was known as the "father of trusts." Although his main trust activity involved South American rubber, he also contributed to the formation of wool, coal, steel, and iron corporations. Flint was chairman of a group which consolidated street railroads in Syracuse; possibly he and Stickley met through their mutual interests in transportation since Stickley had earlier run a street railroad in Binghamton.

14. *Boyd's Syracuse City Directory, 1899–1900,* p. 622.

2 — INFLUENCES FROM EUROPE

1. John Crosby Freeman, *The Forgotten Rebel: Gustav Stickley and His Craftsman Mission Furniture* (Watkins Glen, N.Y.: Century House, 1966), p. 37. Freeman bases his statement on Gustav Stickley, *Chips from the Craftsman Workshops* (New York: Kalkhoff, 1906). Passports were not required for American citizens traveling in Europe prior to 1918, although they were available. According to Ronald E. Swerczek of the National Archives and Records Service, Washington, D.C. (letter, February 23, 1981), there is no record of a passport having been issued to Gustav Stickley in the 1890s.

2. See Chapter 1, p. 6.

3. Freeman, *The Forgotten Rebel*, p. 44. *The Craftsman* 22, no. 3 (June 1912): 302, indicates that Stickley visited Voysey and others "shortly after the first number of *The Craftsman* was issued" which would be in late 1901.

4. Gustav Stickley, "A Plea for a Democratic Art," *The Craftsman* 7 (October 1904): 42; *National Cyclopaedia of American Biography* (New York: James T. White, 1910), 14: 291.

5. John Ruskin, *Seven Lamps of Architecture,* facsimile edition, Noonday Press (New York: Farrar, Straus and Cuday), p. 39.

6. Ruskin, *Seven Lamps,* p. 167.

7. Peter Collins, *Changing Ideals in Modern Architecture* (London: Faber & Faber, 1965), p. 109.

8. John Ruskin, *Stones of Venice* 2, quoted in John D. Rosenberg, *The Genius of John Ruskin, Selections from His Writings* (London: George Allen & Unwin, Ltd., 1963), pp. 180–81.

9. John Ruskin, *Crown of Wild Olives* (1866) quoted in Rosenberg, *The Genius of John Ruskin,* p. 276.

10. J. W. Mackail, *Life of William Morris* (London: Longman, Greene & Co., 1911), 1: 38.

11. William Morris, *Hopes and Fears for Art* (Boston: Roberts Bros., 1897), pp. 66, 32.

12. May Morris, ed., *Collected Works of William Morris* (1910–15), 1: 213–15, quoted in Paul R. Thompson, *The Work of William Morris* (London: Heinemann, 1967), p. 88; and May Morris, *Collected Works of William Morris* 22: 200, quoted in Thompson, *Work of William Morris,* p. 89.

13. Freeman, *The Forgotten Rebel,* p. 17, lists the periodical as being in Stickley's Morris Plains home. The years during which he subscribed to it are unknown.

14. The South Kensington Museum, now the Victoria and Albert Museum, originated as the Museum of Manufactures in 1852. Its mission was the display of decorative art to aid in the improvement of design of British manufactured products.

15. Hermann Muthesius, *Das Englishe Hause* 3 vols. (Berlin: Wasmuth, 1904–1905) republished and abridged as *The English House,* ed. Dennis Sharp and trans. Janet Seligmann (New York: Rizzoli, 1979), p. 194. Muthesius (1861–1927) reported on English house and furniture design for the Prussian Board of Trade. He was technical attaché and later cultural attaché to the German Embassy in London from 1896 to 1903. His research resulted in the publication of *Das Englishe Hause,* an excellent summary of English design during the Arts and Crafts period.

16. Alison Adburgham, "Give the Customers What They Want," *Architectural Review* 141 (May 1977): 295.

17. Isabelle Anscombe and Charlotte Gere, *Arts and Crafts in Britain and America* (New York: Rizzoli, 1978), p. 189; and Victor Arwas, *The Liberty Style* (New York: Rizzoli, 1979), pp. [2–3].

18. See Introduction, p. xii.

19. James D. Kornwolf, *M. H. Baillie Scott and the Arts and Crafts Movement* (Baltimore: Johns Hopkins University Press, 1972), pp. 162–63.

20. See Introduction, p. xiii.

21. Gillian Naylor, *The Arts and Crafts Movement* (Cambridge: MIT Press, 1971), p. 169.

22. Muthesius, *Das Englishe Hause,* p. 31.

23. Irene Sargent, "The Wavy Line," *The Craftsman* 2, no. 3 (1902): 131–42; Josephine C. Locke, "Some Impressions of Art Nouveau," *The Craftsman* 2, no. 4 (1902): 201–204; Irene Sargent, "René Lalique: His Rank among Contemporary Artists," *The Craftsman* 3, no. 2 (1902): 65–73; Alfred D. F. Hamlin, "L'Art Nouveau: Its Origin and Development," *The Craftsman* 3, no. 3 (1902): 129–43; Jean Schopfer and Claude Auet, "L'Art Nouveau: An Argument and Defense in Reply to Professor A. D. F. Hamlin

of Columbia University," *The Craftsman* 4, no. 4 (1903): 229–38; Tristan Destere, "The Workshops and Residence of M. René Lalique," *The Craftsman* 4, no. 1 (1903): 1–8; S[amuel] Bing, "L'Art Nouveau," *The Craftsman* 5, no. 1 (1904): 1–15; Heinrich Pudor, "René Lalique," *The Craftsman* 5, no. 6 (1904): 619–20; A. Grasset, "The Border…," *The Craftsman* 7, no. 4 (1905): 421–30.

24. Robert Koch, "Art Nouveau Bing," *Gazette des Beaux-Arts* 53 (March 1959): 179–80.

25. Barbara Stickley Wiles, interview, February 14, 1979.

26. Koch, "Art Nouveau Bing," pp. 183–94.

27. Samuel Bing, "Wohin Trieben wir?" *Dekorative Kunst* 1 (1898): 1, as quoted in Robert Schmutzler, *Art Nouveau* (New York: Harry N. Abrams, 1962), trans. Edouard Rodite, p. 131.

28. Stickley, *Chips*.

3 — THE BEGINNINGS OF THE CRAFTSMAN EMPIRE

1. Elbert Hubbard (1856–1915) produced furniture at his Roycroft Shops in East Aurora, New York, from 1896 onward. Although furniture production was only a secondary activity of the Roycrofters and they apparently never produced a great quantity of it, some of their designs are of high quality. They were clearly inspired by English Arts and Crafts designers, notably Mackmurdo. Hubbard's primary activity was publication of the *Philistine,* a monthly magazine, and *Little Journies.* As Stickley was to do later, Hubbard produced metal goods in his workshops. See David M. Cathers, *Furniture of the American Arts and Crafts Movement: Stickley and Roycroft Mission Oak* (New York: New American Library, 1981), pp. 85–98.

2. *Catalogue of Craftsman Furniture* (Syracuse: Craftsman Publishing Co., 1910), pp. 3–4.

3. *American Cabinet Maker and Upholsterer* (June 30, 1900), quoted by Cathers, *Furniture,* p. 34 n. 3.

4. Margaret Edgewood, "Some Sensible Furniture," *The House Beautiful* 8, no. 5 (October 1900): 653–55.

5. The Yokohama plant stand illustrated in the Tobey advertisement has a Grueby tile insert. The Grueby Faience Company, established in 1894, had a continuing relationship with Gustav Stickley who used Grueby tile in his Craftsman interiors and illustrated Grueby ceramics in *The Craftsman.* Stickley and Grueby presented a joint exhibit at the Buffalo Pan American Exposition in 1901. See Martin Eidelberg, "Art Pottery-Grueby," in Robert Judson Clark, ed., *The Arts and Crafts Movement in America, 1876–1916* (Princeton: Princeton University Press, 1972), p. 136.

6. *American Cabinet Maker and Upholsterer* (December 22, 1900), noted in Cathers, *Furniture,* p. 38.

7. Evamaria Hardin, "The Architectural Legacy of Archimedes Russell" (M.A. thesis, Syracuse University, 1979), pp. 229–32.

8. Irene Sargent, "A Recent Arts and Crafts Exhibition," *The Craftsman* 4, no. 2 (May 1903): 69–83.

9. Although John Crosby Freeman, *The Forgotten Rebel: Gustav Stickley and His Craftsman Mission Furniture* (Watkins Glen, N.Y.: Century House, 1966), p. 16, and Cathers, *Furniture,* p. 38, state that Stickley bought the Crouse Stables, he did not. It was owned by Charles M. Warner until 1904, then briefly by Arthur Realty Company, and bought by the Independent Telephone Company in 1905 according to "Tax Records, Fifteenth Ward," City of Syracuse, 1900–1905. It was demolished in 1936.

10. *Boyd's Syracuse City Directory, 1902* (Syracuse: Boyd, 1902), p. 940, lists the Orleans Sand

Stone Company, Syracuse Improvements Company, G. E. Warner and Company, and Warner-Quinlan Asphalt Company as sharing the Crouse Stables.

11. Sargent, "A Recent Arts and Crafts Exhibition," pp. 69–83.

12. A variation of the Celantine tea table called the Poppy table was illustrated earlier in the Chicago *Tribune* (October 7, 1900), its only differences being that it had a flowerlike lower shelf rather than crossed stretchers and that it had a weathered oak finish.

13. Cathers, *Furniture,* p. 144.

14. Ibid., p. 204.

15. Peter Wiles, interview, July 22, 1980.

16. George F. Clingman to Leopold Stickley, May 26, 1911, Stickley Collection, Archives and Research Library, Edison Institute, Henry Ford Museum and Greenfield Village, Dearborn, Michigan.

17. Cathers, *Furniture,* pp. 12–15.

18. See Introduction, pp. xi–xiii.

19. John Crosby Freeman's *The Forgotten Rebel: Gustav Stickley and His Craftsman Mission Furniture* (Watkins Glen, N.Y.: Century House, 1966), pp. 66–98, contains a useful author index to *The Craftsman* with biographical information on some of the authors. For the Syracuse years of *The Craftsman,* 1901–1906, see Sally J. Kinsey, "Gustav Stickley and the Early Years of *The Craftsman*" (M.A. thesis, Syracuse University, 1972). For representative excerpts from *The Craftsman,* see Barry Sanders, ed., *The Craftsman, an Anthology* (Santa Barbara and Salt Lake City: Peregrine Smith, 1978).

20. Gustav Stickley, "Thoughts Occasioned by an Anniversary, A Plea for a Democratic Art," *The Craftsman* 7, no. 1 (October 1904): 57.

21. Cleota Reed Gabriel, "Irene Sargent: Rediscovering a Lost Legend," *Courier* 14, no. 2 (Summer 1979): 4–9. See also Cleota Reed, "Irene Sargent: A Comprehensive Bibliography of Her Published Writings," *Courier* 18, no. 1 (Spring 1981): 10–17.

22. Irene Sargent, "William Morris, His Socialistic Career," *The Craftsman* 1, no. 1 (October 1901): 9, 17–18, 20.

23. Irene Sargent, "A Chapter from Prince Kropotkin's 'Mutual Aid in the Medieval City,'" *The Craftsman* 4, no. 3 (June 1903): 209–220. Kropotkin was a Russian geographer, author, and revolutionary who advocated anarchy. After being imprisoned several times for spreading revolutionary propaganda, he settled in England to write. He returned to Russia in 1917, and lived there until his death, taking no part in politics.

24. Gustav Stickley, "Als Ik Kan — Cooperation of Employer and Employed as a Solution of Socialism and the Labor Problem," *The Craftsman* 15, no. 5 (February 1909): 620–21. Gustav Stickley wrote a *Craftsman* editor's column called "Chips from the Craftsman's Workshop" until April 1905. In July 1905, he began to call his column "Als Ik Kan" after his motto.

25. Oscar L. Triggs, "The Workshop and School," *The Craftsman* 3, no. 1 (October 1902): 21, 28–29. Triggs was a professor at the University of Chicago, secretary of the Industrial Arts League at Chicago, and author of *Chapters in the History of the Arts and Crafts Movement* (1902). The manual training movement, European in origin, reached the United States in the last quarter of the nineteenth century. See Melvin L. Barlow, *History of Industrial Education in the United States* (Peoria: Bennett, 1967); and Lewis F. Anderson, *History of Manual and Industrial School Education* (New York and London: Appleton, 1926).

26. Vivian Burnett, "Craftsman Gardens for Craftsman Houses," *The Craftsman* 18, no. 1 (April 1910): 46–58.

27. Eloise Roorbach, "A Japanese Garden in America: Garden-Making that in Formal Manner Expresses History, Romance and Poetry," *The Craftsman* 26, no. 6 (March 1915): 620–29.

28. M. L. Wakeman Curtis, "How Beauty and Labor Are Interwoven in the Daily Life of Japan," *The Craftsman* 17, no. 5 (February 1910): 517.

29. Kathryn Rucker, "Japan's Beauty as an Inspiration to American Home-Builders," *The Craftsman* 24, no. 4 (April 1913): 42–51.

30. Gustav Stickley, "The Colorado Desert and California," *The Craftsman* 6, no. 3 (June 1904): 247.

31. Constance Goddard DuBois, "The Indian Woman as Craftsman," *The Craftsman* 6, no. 4 (July 1904): 393.

32. Gustav Stickley, "Nature and Art in California," *The Craftsman* 6, no. 4 (July 1904): 370–72. Stickley was not alone in his admiration for California mission architecture. See Karen Jeanine Weitze, *Origins and Early Development of Mission Revival in California* (Ph.D. diss., Stanford University, 1977, as reproduced by University Microfilms International, Ann Arbor, 1978).

33. George Wharton James, "The Influence of the 'Mission Style' upon the Civic and Domestic Architecture of Modern California," *The Craftsman* 5, no. 4 (January 1904): 458–69. James wrote a number of *Craftsman* articles on mission architecture and Indian life. He later moved to California, where he published one issue of a journal, *Arroya Craftsman,* in 1909. In this issue he acknowledged Stickley as the "original Craftsman, ... the founder, proprietor and editor of that great exponent of the Simple Life and of Democratic Art — *The Craftsman* magazine." See Timothy J. Anderson, Eudorah M. Moore, and Robert W. Winters, eds., *California Design 1910* (Pasadena: California Design Publications, 1974).

4 — THE CRAFTSMAN EMPIRE EXPANDS

1. The street number was originally 416, and the house was the first to be built on the block according to "Tax Records, Seventeenth Ward," City of Syracuse, 1900, Block 580, Lot 11, Rosenbloom Tract. Stickley's tax rate rose in June 1900, an indication that the house was then complete rather than under construction. The street number was changed in 1918.

2. Baillie Scott's "Winscombe," published in *Academy Architecture* (1900) had both features as did Voysey's "Lodge for a Manchester Suburb," in *British Architecture* (May 28, 1890). Voysey's Forster House (plate 5) has a similar bay window as did Baillie Scott's "Country House" in *Stuido* (February 1900).

3. M. H. Baillie Scott, "A Small Country House," *International Studio* 3, no. 2 (January 1898): 172.

4. Robert C. Spencer, "Work of Frank Lloyd Wright," *Architectural Review* 7, no. 5 (May 1900), n.s. 2, no. 5: 61–72.

5. See Chapter 3, p. 24.

6. For examples of the house plans of the 1870s and '80s with the living hall, see Vincent J. Scully, Jr., *The Shingle Style and the Stick Style,* rev. ed. (New Haven: Yale University Press, 1971).

7. Samuel Howe, "A Visit to the House of Mr. Stickley," *The Craftsman* 3, no. 3 (February 1903): 166, 168–69.

8. Peter Wiles, interview, April 26, 1981.

9. Irene Sargent, "A House and a Home," *The Craftsman* 2, no. 5 (August 1902): 242–45.

10. Stickley may have been inspired by Baillie Scott's St. Amory house published in *The Building News* (May 10, 1895) and his Schlobach house, also in *The Building News* (October 29, 1897).

11. "The Craftsman House," *The Craftsman* 4, no. 2 (May 1903): 84–92.

12. Much has been written about Harvey Ellis. Some of the most important sources are: Claude Bragdon, "Harvey Ellis: A Portrait Sketch," *Architectural Review* 15, no. 12 (December 1908); David Cathers, *Genius in the Shadows, The Furniture Designs of Harvey Ellis* (New York: Jordan Volpe Gallery, 1981); Hugh M. G. Garden, "Harvey Ellis, Designer and Draftsman," *Architectural Review* 15, no. 12 (December 1908); Roger Kennedy, "Long Dark Corridors: Harvey Ellis," *Prairie School Review* 5 (First Quarter, 1968): 5–18; Jean France, "Harvey Ellis, 'Architect,' " *A Rediscovery — Harvey Ellis: Artist, Architect* (Rochester: Memorial Art Gallery of the University of Rochester and Margaret Woodbury Strong Museum, 1972); Barry Sanders, "Harvey Ellis: Architect, Painter, Furniture Designer," *Art and Antiques* 4, no. 1 (January–February 1981): 58–67. The Bragdon and Garden articles were reprinted in *Prairie School Review* 5 (First Quarter 1968).

13. Kennedy, "Long Dark Corridors," 8–13.

14. Bragdon, "Harvey Ellis," *Prairie School Review,* p. 22. Claude Bragdon (1866–1946) began his architectural career in Charles Ellis' office. He wrote a number of books on theosophy and architecture. Bragman may have introduced Ellis to Stickley for whose *Craftsman* he had written two articles in 1903.

15. William G. Purcell, "Forgotten Builders — the Nation's Voice," *Northwest Architect* 8, nos. 6–7 (1944): 5, as quoted by Kennedy, "Long Dark Corridors," p. 8.

16. Claude Bradgon, *More Lives Than One* (New York: Alfred A. Knopf, 1938), p. 41.

17. Bragdon, "Harvey Ellis," *Prairie School Review,* p. 23.

18. France, "Harvey Ellis, 'Architect,' " p. 7.

19. Bragdon, "Harvey Ellis," *Prairie School Review,* p. 21.

20. Harvey Ellis, "Craftsman House," *Craftsman* 4, no. 4 (July 1903): 274–75.

21. This window design was executed for use above the built-in sideboard in Dumblane, the Craftsman house of Hazen Bond in Washington, D.C. See Chapter 5, pp. 101–105. Also see *The Craftsman* 23, no. 5 (February 1912): 528 for a photograph of the stained glass window.

22. Kennedy, "Long Dark Corridors," p. 14.

23. Harvey Ellis, "Sermons in Sun Dried Brick. From the Old Spanish Missions," *The Craftsman* 5, no. 3 (December 1903): 212–16.

24. "Puss in Boots, An Old Myth in New Dress," *The Craftsman* 4, no. 5 (August 1903): 371–83.

25. "Structure and Ornament in the Craftsman Workshops," *The Craftsman* 5, no. 4 (January 1904): 392, 394, 396.

26. David M. Cathers, *Furniture of the American Arts and Crafts Movement: Stickley and Roycroft Mission Oak* (New York: New American Library, 1981), p. 148. Stickley received patents #37507 and #37508 for his spindle chair frames in 1905.

5 — THE CRAFTSMAN HOME BUILDERS' CLUB

1. Barry Sanders, ed., *The Best of Craftsman Homes* (Sanata Barbara and Salt Lake City: Peregrine Smith, 1979), p. vii.

2. "Craftsman House: Series of 1906, Number II," *The Craftsman* 9 (October 1905, March 1906): 713–17.

3. Anthony King, "The Bungalow in India: Its Regional and Pre-Industrial Origin," *Architectural Association Quarterly* 5, no. 3 (July–September 1973): 8–18.

4. For a general study of the American bungalow, see Clay Lancaster, "The American Bungalow," *Art Bulletin* 40 (September 1958): 239–53. See Robert Winter, *The California Bungalow* (Los Angeles: Hennessey and Ingalls, 1980), for a more specific study of bungalows in California and elsewhere.

5. See Chapter 3, pp. 42–43.

6. "Cool and Quiet Days," *The Craftsman* 6, no. 2 (July 1904): 402–406.

7. "Designs for Craftsman Rural Dwellings," *The Craftsman* 15, no. 4 (January 1909): 718. This house was also published in Gustav Stickley's *Craftsman Homes* (New York: Craftsman Publishing Company, 1909), pp. 42–44, with a slightly different text.

8. Una Nixon Hopkins, "The Development of Domestic Architecture on the Pacific Coast," *The Craftsman* 13, no. 4 (January 1908): 455. Helen Lukens Gaut also reported regularly on California architecture in *The Craftsman*.

9. "Designs for Craftsman Rural Dwellings," *The Craftsman* 15, no. 6 (March 1909): 718–22. This house was also published in Stickley, *Craftsman Homes,* pp. 66–67.

10. Laura Rinkle Johnson, "The Little House in the Orchard," *The Craftsman* 24, no. 3 (June 1913): 331–33. The J. Gordon Smyth house in Van Lear, Kentucky, was also built from this plan. See "A Craftsman House Built on a Kentucky Hillside," *The Craftsman* 23, no. 1 (October 1912): 104–106.

11. H. Allen Brooks, *The Prairie School, Frank Lloyd Wright and his Midwest Contemporaries* (New York: W. W. Norton, 1972), pp. 34–35.

12. "The Evolution of a Hillside Home: Raymond Riordon's Indiana Bungalow," *The Craftsman* 25, no. 1 (October 1913): 48–55.

13. Mr. Garritt's name is listed as C. O. Garrett in *The Craftsman* 26, no. 5 (August 1914): 545, in "Craftsman Houses Large and Small," an article on houses built to Craftsman plans. Local town records list him as Chauncey C. Garrett or Garritt.

14. "A Craftsman Cottage and Bungalow for Homebuilders of Simple Needs and Tastes," *The Craftsman* 23, no. 3 (December 1912): 336–41.

15. "Craftsman Wood and Stone Bungalows for the Country," *The Craftsman* 20, no. 2 (May 1911): 199–204. This house was also published in *Twenty-four Craftsman Houses with Floor Plans* (New York: The Craftsman, 1910).

16. See "The Craftsman Fireplace: More Details about This Heating and Ventilating System," *The Craftsman* 21, no. 1 (April 1912): 109–110.

17. "Dumblane, a Southern Craftsman Home," *The Craftsman* 23, no. 5 (February 1912): 522–34.

18. "Craftsman House, Series of 1904, Number X," *The Craftsman* no. 1 (October 1904): 75–87.

19. "Dumblane," pp. 526–28.

20. "The Cost of the Craftsman House: Why These Designs Do Not Lend Themselves to What Is Called 'Cheap Building,'" *The Craftsman* 17, no. 6 (March 1910): 681.

6 — OTHER CRAFTSMAN HOUSES

1. "Ledger 1901–05," 76 × 101.11, p. 114, and subsequent apartment rent entries, "Business Papers of Gustav Stickley," Henry Francis Dupont Winterthur Museum, Winterthur, Delaware. Hereafter cited as Winterthur.

2. Gustav Stickley, "The Colorado Desert and California," *The Craftsman* 6, no. 4 (June 1904): 253.

3. [Gustav Stickley], "The Craftsman House: A Practical Application of All the Theories of Home Building Advocated in This Magazine," *The Craftsman* 15, no. 1 (October 1908): 79.

4. Ibid., pp. 80, 85–87.

5. "The Club House at Craftsman Farms: A Log House Planned Especially for the Entertainment of Guests," *The Craftsman* 15, no. 3 (December 1908): 339.

6. "Craftsman Log Houses: Series of 1908, No. III," *The Craftsman* 11, no. 6 (March 1907): 742–55.

7. "Private Ledger, Gustav Stickley Personal, 1910–12," April 26–July 6, 1910, 76 × 101.54, Winterthur.

8. Natalie Curtis, "The New Log House at Craftsman Farms: An Architectural Development of the Log Cabin," *The Craftsman* 21, no. 2 (November 1911): 201.

9. See Chapter, 5, pp. 96–97, 176 n. 16.

10. Raymond Riordon, "A Visit to Craftsman Farms: The Impression It Made and the Results: The Gustav Stickley School for Citizenship," *The Craftsman* 23, no. 2 (November 1912): 152–58. See also "Craftsman Farms: Its Development and Future," *The Craftsman* 25, no. 1 (December 1913): 8–15. For Riordon's Craftsman house in Rolling Prairie, Indiana, see Chapter 5, p 94.

11. "Some Craftsman Houses That Were Built Under Our Own Supervision," *The Craftsman* 18, no. 6 (September 1910): 662, 665–66. The following houses are discussed in the article: W. H. Phillips house, Whitestone, N.Y.; E. L. Prior house, Maplewood, N.J.; Frederick M. Hill house, Great Neck, N.Y.; B. A. Taylor house, Summit, N.J.

12. Interview, present owners of B. A. Taylor house, Summit, N.J., July 1977.

13. "Some Craftsman Houses That Were Built Under Our Own Supervision," p. 671.

14. "A Craftsman House that Is Being Built for a Physician on the Garden City Estates, Garden City, Long Island," *The Craftsman* 16, no. 2 (May 1909): x, xii, xiv.

15. "A Craftsman House That Is Being Built for a Physician," p. x.

16. "Cash Receipts and Disbursements, July 1, 1909–July 15, 1910," 76 × 101.4578, pp. 34–35, Winterthur.

17. Although many volumes of Gustav Stickley's business records still exist at Winterthur, they are unhelpful in identifying the individual draftsman and/or designers who were the Craftsman architects.

18. See Chapter 5, pp. 96, 101–105.

19. "The Value of Coöperation between Owner and Architect as Illustrated by Specially Designed Craftsman Homes," *The Craftsman* 24, no 1 (April 1913): 69–78. Other custom designed houses discussed are the E. B. Shiebe house, Cambridge, Mass., and the E. J. Wagner house, Smithtown, N.Y.

20. The drawings for the Bronson house, now in Avery Architectural and Fine Arts Library, Columbia University, New York, N.Y., are dated 3/4/14.

21. See Chapter 5, pp. 87, 91.

22. "Drawings, Charles B. Evans house," Avery Architectural and Fine Arts Library, Columbia University, New York, N.Y. The drawings are dated 1914.

7 — *THE CRAFTSMAN,* RECOGNITION OF ARCHITECTS, AND PLANNING

1. Frederick Stymetz Lamb, "Modern Use of the Gothic: The Possibilities of New Architectural Style," *The Craftsman* 8, no. 2 (May 1905): 150–70.

2. A. D. F. Hamlin, "Style in Architecture," *The Craftsman* 8, no. 3 (June 1905): 325–31.

3. Bertram C. Goodhue, "The Romantic Point of View," *The Craftsman* 8, no. 3 (June 1905): 332–33.

4. Samuel Howe, "The Architectural Awakening," *The Craftsman* 8, no. 3 (June 1905): 333–35.

5. Louis H. Sullivan, "Reply to Mr. Frederick Stymetz Lamb on 'Modern Use of Gothic: The Possibility of New Architectural Style,'" *The Craftsman* 8, no. 3 (June 1905): 336–38.

6. Louis H. Sullivan, "The Architectural Discussion: Form and Function Artistically Considered," *The Craftsman* 8, no. 4 (July 1905): 453.

7. Ibid., p. 457.

8. Carl K. Bennett, "A Bank Built for Farmers: Louis Sullivan Designs a Building Which Marks a New Epoch in American Architecture," *The Craftsman* 15, no. 2 (November 1908): 176–85.

9. William Gray Purcell and George H. Elmslie, "The American Renaissance," *The Craftsman* 21, no. 4 (January 1912): 430–35. For information on Purcell and Elmslie, see David Gebhard, *The Work of Purcell and Elmslie* (Park Forest, Ill.: Prairie School Press, 1965), intro., which is a reprint of three special issues on their work in *Western Architect.*

10. Ibid., p. 434.

11. Founded in 1897, the Chicago Arts and Crafts Society was the first such group in the United States. See H. Allen Brooks, *The Prairie School, Frank Lloyd Wright and his Midwest Contemporaries* (New York: W. W. Norton & Co., 1976), p. 17.

12. Margaret Edgewood, "Some Sensible Furniture," *The House Beautiful* 8, no. 5 (October 1900): 653–55. See Chapter 3, p. 24.

13. "Wilson Eyre: A Pioneer in American Domestic Architecture," *The Craftsman* 18, no. 3 (June 1909): 367. Wilson Eyre, a member of Stickley's generation and thus older than Wright, Purcell, and Elmslie, practiced in and near Philadelphia. Although his early work was in the Shingle style, his mature designs are related to English Arts and Crafts architecture. He was one of the first American Arts and Crafts architects. Eyre was a founder of *House and Garden* and its editor 1901–1906. See James D. Kornwolf, *M. H. Baillie Scott and the Arts and Crafts Movement* (Baltimore: Johns Hopkins University Press, 1972), pp. 349–53, for a discussion of Eyre's relation to the Arts and Crafts Movement.

14. Frederick Wallick, "The Rational Art of Wilson Eyre, an Architect Who Designs Houses to Meet the Needs and Express the Qualities of Today," *The Craftsman* 17, no. 5 (February 1910): 537–51.

15. Wilson Eyre, "American Country Houses of Today: An Achievement in Domestic Architecture," *The Craftsman* 24, no. 1 (April 1913): 21–22.

16. Henrietta P. Keith, "The Trail of Japanese Influence in Our Modern Domestic Architecture," *The Craftsman* 12, no. 4 (July 1907): 446–51.

See Randell L. Mackinson, *Greene and Greene: Architecture as a Fine Art* (Santa Barbara and Salt Lake City: Peregrine Smith, Inc., 1977). For a shorter introduction to Greene and Greene, see Mackinson, "Greene and Greene," in Esther McCoy, *Five California Architects* (New York: Praeger, 1975), pp. 102–147.

17. "California's Contribution to a National Architecture: Its Significance and Beauty as Shown in the Work of Greene and Greene, Architects," *The Craftsman* 22, no. 5 (August 1912): 533. See also "Your Own House: Number Six: The Approach to the House," *The Craftsman* 28, no. 2 (May 1915): 202–210.

18. Ibid., p. 536.

19. Ibid., p. 547.

20. Eloise Roorbach, " 'Outdoor' Life in California Houses, as Expressed in the New Architecture of Irving J. Gill," *The Craftsman* 24, no. 4 (July 1913): 437. See also by Roorbach on Gill: "The Garden Apartments of California," *Architectural Record* 24 (December 1913): 518–30, and "Celebrating Simplicity in Architecture," *Western Architect* 19 (April 1913): 35–38. Irving Gill was born in Syracuse, New York, where his father was a contractor. He moved to Chicago in 1890, and worked for Louis Sullivan until 1893, when he moved on to San Diego, California. See McCoy, *Five California Architects,* pp. 58–100 for a survey of his work in California.

21. Irving J. Gill, "The Home of the Future: The New Architecture of the West: Small Homes for a Great Country: Number Four," *The Craftsman* 30, no. 2 (May 1916): 142.

22. William H. Jordy, *American Buildings and Their Architects* vol. 3, *Progressive and Academic Ideals at the Turn of the Century* (Garden City: Anchor/Doubleday, 1976), p. 247.

23. Roorbach, " 'Outdoor' Life," p. 438.

24. Barry Parker, "Modern Country Homes in England: Number Three," *The Craftsman* 18, no. 3 (June 1910): 324–34.

25. Walter L. Creese, "Parker and Unwin: Architects of Totality," *Journal of the Society of Architectural Historians* 22 (October 1963): 162–63.

26. Mabel Luke Priestman, "A Co-operative Village for Working People—Beautiful and Practical

27. Raymond Unwin, "The Improvement of Towns," *The Craftsman* 8, no. 6 (September 1905): 809–816. The idea of the garden city, of which Letchworth was the first example, originated with Ebenezer Howard. His book, *Garden Cities of Tomorrow* (1901), originally called *Tomorrow, A Peaceful Path to Real Reform,* expounded a theory of new towns to relieve urban congestion. Parker and Unwin designed Letchworth generally according to Howard's principles and with his guidance. See Walter L. Creese, *The Search for Environment, The Garden City: Before and After* (New Haven: Yale University Press, 1966), and the whole issue of *Architectural Review* 166, no. 976 (June 1978), which is devoted to the Garden City Movement.

28. [Gustav Stickley], "Rapid Growth of the Garden City Movement, Which Promises to Reorganize Social Conditions All Over the World," *The Craftsman* 17, no. 3 (December 1909): 296.

29. Ibid., pp. 309–310. One of the articles in Barry Parker's "Modern Country Homes in England" series, no. 23, *The Craftsman* 22, no. 1 (April 1912): 54–65, discusses the advantages for single men and women of cooperative apartments with common kitchens, dining rooms, living rooms, laundries, and servants' quarters. It is illustrated with a Belgian apartment complex and terrace house plans.

30. Edward Hale Brush, "A Garden City for the Man of Moderate Means," *The Craftsman* 19, no. 5 (February 1911): 445–51.

31. Frank Choutau Brown, "Civic Improvement in Boston…," *The Craftsman* 19, no. 3 (December 1910): 273–83, and "Progress in Civic Improvements in Boston," *The Craftsman* 24, no. 6 (September 1913): 599–610; Charles Harcourt Ainslie Forbes-Lindsay, "Great Falls: The Pioneer Park City of Montana," *The Craftsman* 15, no. 2 (November 1908): 200–209; Marion Craig Wentworth, "A Civic Center of Real Beauty for the People of Santa Barbara," *The Craftsman* 27, no. 3 (December 1914): 320–33.

8 — THE COLLAPSE OF THE CRAFTSMAN EMPIRE

1. *The Craftsman* 25, no. 4 (January 1914): 8a, inside back cover.

2. David A. Hanks, "Chicago and the Midwest," in Robert Judson Clark, ed., *The Arts and Crafts Movement in America 1876–1916* (Princeton: Princeton University Press, 1972), p. 7.

3. See Chapter, 1, p. 2.

4. *American Cabinet Maker and Upholsterer* (February 1, 1902) as quoted in David M. Cathers, *Furniture of the American Arts and Crafts Movement: Stickley and Roycroft Mission Oak* (New York: New American Library, 1981), pp. 70–71. Although Leopold Stickley celebrated his fiftieth anniversary as a furniture manufacturer in 1950, he was two years premature unless he was counting the period in which he worked for Gustav. Local tax records indicate that Leopold and J. George Stickley purchased their factory from L. L. Chapman in 1902 (Grantee Index, Series 3, Onondaga County, 1901 and later, p. 2405). They continued to add to their factory property throughout the 1910s.

5. Cathers, *Furniture,* pp. 84 n. 1, 77.

6. *The Work of L. and J. G. Stickley, Fayetteville, New York,* n.d.

7. Gustav Stickley, "Als Ik Kan: The Craftsman's Birthday Party," *The Craftsman* 24, no. 2 (May 1913): 252.

8. "Lease for 6 E. 39th Street," 76 × 101.2355, "Business Papers of Gustav Stickley," Henry Francis Dupont Winterthur Museum, Winterthur, Delaware. Hereafter cited as Winterthur.

9. For a fuller description of the New York Craftsman Building, see "Furnishing the Home: The Opportunity Afforded by the New Craftsman Building," *The Craftsman* 25, no. 3 (December 1913): 299–303, and "The Craftsman Restaurant: by a Visitor," *The Craftsman* 25, no. 4 (January 1914): 362–68, 397–98. The contents for the Craftsman Building were dispersed in a bankruptcy sale in 1918; Stickley descendants have some souvenirs of the building which is still standing.

10. Barbara Stickley Wiles, tape recording, 1979.

11. Edward S. Wood to Howard E. Brown, 20 January 1913, 76 × 101.2356, Winterthur.

12. "Craftsman Publishing Company Tax Return, 1913," 76 × 101.2391, Winterthur.

13. See Chapter 6, pp. 127, 131.

14. Gustav Stickley, *Craftsman Furniture* (Syracuse: Craftsman Publishing Co., 1912).

15. "More Color in the Home: Painted Furniture Inspired by Peasant Art," *The Craftsman* 28, no. 2 (June 1915): 245–52.

16. Gustav Stickley, "Furniture Based upon Good Craftsmanship," *The Craftsman* 29, no. 5 (February 1916): 531. For a discussion of "Colonial" revival furniture by Stickley and others see William B. Rhoads, *The Colonial Revival* 1 (Ph.D. diss., Princeton University, 1974; reprint ed., Outstanding Dissertations in the Fine Arts, New York: Garland Publishing Co., 1977), pp. 344–89.

17. "Four Popular Craftsman Plans," *The Craftsman* 30, no. 6 (September 1916): 647.

18. "Minutes of The Craftsman, Inc., 7 October 1912–6 April 1914," p. 42, and "Minutes of The Craftsman, Inc., 27 June 1914–2 February 1915," p. 211.

19. Howard E. Brown, secretary, The Craftsman, Inc. to Secretary of Clerk of District Court, Boston, 23 March 1915, 76 × 101.2358, Winterthur.

20. Howard E. Brown, secretary, The Craftsman, Inc. to all accounts receivable, 20 May 1915, 76 × 101.2359, Winterthur.

21. Howard E. Brown, secretary, The Craftsman, Inc. to Howard P. Denison, 1 August 1915, 76 × 101.230, Winterthur.

22. John Crosby Freeman, *The Forgotten Rebel: Gustav Stickley and His Craftsman Mission Furniture* (Watkins Glen, N.Y.: Century House, 1966), p. 19.

23. Cathers, *Furniture,* pp. 80–82.

24. Barbara Stickley Wiles, tape recording, 1979.

25. Freeman, *The Forgotten Rebel,* p. 20.

26. Barbara Stickley Wiles, tape recording, 1979.

27. See *Stickley Craftsman Furniture Catalogs* with an introduction by David M. Cathers (New York: Dover Publications, 1979); Stephen Gray and Robert Edwards, eds., *Collected Works of Gustav Stickley* (New York: Turn of the Century Editions, 1981); Barry Sanders, ed., *The Craftsman, An Anthology* (Santa Barbara: Peregrine Smith, 1978); Gustav Stickley, *Craftsman Homes* (Syracuse: Craftsman Publishing Co., 1909; reprint ed. New York: Dover Publishing Co., 1979); and Barry Sanders, ed., *Best of Craftsman Homes* (Santa Barbara: Peregrine Smith, 1979).

28. Gustav Stickley, "The Craftsman Movement: Its Origin and Growth," *The Craftsman* 25, no. 1 (October 1913). 17–18, 23–26.

29. Robert Judson Clark, ed., *The Arts and Crafts Movement in America 1876–1916* (Princeton: Princeton University Press, 1972), pp. 39, 59.

30. See Chapter 5, p. 94.

31. For a more extensive list of bungalow books, see Robert Winter, *The California Bungalow* (Los Angeles: Hennessey and Ingalls, 1980).

INDEX

185

GUSTAV STICKLEY, THE CRAFTSMAN

was composed in eleven-point Merganthaler VIP Garamond Book and leaded one point
by Utica Typesetting Company, Inc.,
with display type in Windsor composed on the Typositor and condensed
by Dix Typesetting Co., Inc.;
printed on 60-pound, acid-free Warren Old Style Wove,
Smythe-sewn and bound over boards with Joanna Arrestox B,
by Maple-Vail Book Manufacturing Group, Inc.;

and published by
SYRACUSE UNIVERSITY PRESS
SYRACUSE, NEW YORK 13210